LOWER ED

LOWER ED

THE TROUBLING RISE
OF FOR-PROFIT COLLEGES
IN THE NEW ECONOMY

Tressie McMillan Cottom

THE NEW PRESS

25 YEARS

NEW YORK
LONDON

Requests for permission to reproduce selections from this book should be mailed to:
Permissions Department, The New Press, 120 Wall Street, 31st floor, New York, NY 10005.

Published in the United States by The New Press, New York, 2017
Distributed by Perseus Distribution

ISBN 978-1-62097-060-7 (hc)
ISBN 978-1-62097-102-4 (e-book)
CIP data is available

The New Press publishes books that promote and enrich public discussion and
understanding of the issues vital to our democracy and to a more equitable world. These
books are made possible by the enthusiasm of our readers; the support of a committed group
of donors, large and small; the collaboration of our many partners in the independent media
and the not-for-profit sector; booksellers, who often hand-sell New Press books; librarians;
and above all by our authors.

www.thenewpress.com

Composition by Dix!
This book was set in Garamond Premier Pro

Printed in the United States of America

10 9 8 7 6 5 4 3 2 1

For everyone trying to make a dollar out of 15 cents,
but especially for the sisters.

CONTENTS

LOWER ED

INTRODUCTION:
THE EDUCATION GOSPEL

In the first decade of the twenty-first century, as millions of Americans entered higher education, almost 30 percent of them went to for-profit colleges, and I enrolled at least a couple hundred of those students.[1] I worked first at a cosmetology school and later at a technical college. I remember many of those students—their stories, their struggles, their daily successes—but Jason is the student who most changed my life. When I think of Jason now, I hope that he can't say the same of my impact on him.

When we met, Jason was in his early twenties. He was a local boy, born and raised in a rural suburb of Charlotte, North Carolina. At the time, Charlotte was a thriving urban core in the U.S. South. Its national stature, good quality of life, and strong labor markets relied significantly on the banking industry. As the banks went, so too went Charlotte's economic fortunes. When I met Jason, the banks were post–technology bubble but pre–global recession. I was an enrollment officer at the Technical College. It was one of a dozen for-profit colleges in the Charlotte area, each with slightly different branding. There was the for-profit college in high-end Southpark that only offered graduate degrees in business and technology. There was the all-male for-profit college over by the airport whose claim to fame was training mechanics to work at NASCAR. Then there were for-profit colleges in cosmetology, barbering, and what we would have once called secretarial programs. Like those other brands, the Technical College was located in a business park. This one was sandwiched between the high-end part of town and the growing middle-class subdivisions filling up with black and Hispanic families using low down-payment mortgages to escape the center city. The entire school occupied two floors of a six-story building. I had worked previously in a similar role at a cosmetology school (see Chapter 2). Unlike the cosmetology school, the Technical College offered degrees instead of certificates: associate's, bachelor's, and master's degrees in technology, business, and criminal justice. Technology and business were very broadly defined. Technology included a program in electrical engineering that emphasized electrical more than engineering. The students learned business technology and how to wire common electrical units like those in household appliances instead of learning the math of engineering a structure with electricity. The business degree was "applied," meaning it included everything from how to write a business memo to how to use accounting software like Quicken. The master's in business also included case studies in common business problems like managing bad publicity. Only the criminal justice curriculum was occupationally specific. The course had to qualify students to take the police exam, and, as a result, it had the most valuable real estate in the building. One entire classroom was set up like a crime scene.

When students like Jason came to visit, anyone who couldn't name a specific occupational interest or degree program was steered to technology or business. Only students who specifically asked for criminal justice were given information about that program. If you didn't know what you wanted a degree in or what kind of job you hoped to have, technology and business were deemed suitably general enough to tell you how much you'd like them but specific enough to sound like something you heard on the news was a "good job." Jason didn't know what he wanted a degree in, so I told him about technology and business. He chose technology because, he said, "I always upgrade my phone."

Jason was newly married to his high school sweetheart, Bree, who attended each of his appointments with him. They held hands and prayed together before he enrolled. He was eloquent and earnest. They were members of one of the area's non-denominational megachurches that met in shopping centers and played rock music during worship. Between them, Jason and Bree had one truck, three jobs, and one high school diploma. She was working part-time and hoping to work full-time. They wanted a family and thought God was leading them to adopt a Kenyan child with special needs, as friends in their congregation had done. Jason had graduated from high school but suffered from severe test anxiety, which had caught up with him when he once enrolled in community college.

Jason's test anxiety was common enough among prospective students at the Technical College. It was also a potential roadblock to the stated purpose of my job—closing the sale and helping the economy (more on this later)—because the Technical College required an online skills test during the enrollment process. This was fairly rare among for-profit colleges, most of which have very few admission criteria (they are typically called open-access schools). The Technical College used something called the Wonderlic Cognitive Ability Test, best known for being the test that the National Football League uses to assess the IQ of new players.[2] The fifty-question assessment purports to scale group intelligence scores and peg them to the average school grade. For example, a 20 on the Wonderlic is roughly equivalent to a 100 on an IQ test, or the baseline for "average intelligence." The Technical College paid for a version of the Wonderlic that then correlated the IQ score with scholastic skill levels and provided a General Assessment of Instructional Needs (GAIN) score. For example, if this score were a 5, it meant that the test taker had the IQ of the typical fifth grader. To "pass," prospective students at the Technical College had to score at least a 6. Prospective students could take the online assessment as many times as necessary to get a 6, and scores generally improved the more the test was taken. If all else failed, ambitious enrollment officers coached prospective students to make sure they passed. There was no real chance of failure. We never told the prospective student that. Instead, passing the Wonderlic became part of the motivational sales technique.

Jason was terrified of the Wonderlic. Per the instructions in the training manual, I told Jason that he could take the entrance test multiple times until he passed. On his first try, Jason just barely made the cut-off score. He was stunned. Bree beamed. Then I told him what my supervisor had instructed us to tell those who passed: even she, who was enrolled in an MBA program at another local for-profit college, had failed it her first time. The point was that someone like Jason should be proud of his accomplishment and confident enough in his academic future to complete the financial aid paperwork. Happy to have cleared an academic bar he'd previously failed and anxious to earn a degree for a good job to support a young family, Jason had toured the campus, paid his enrollment fee, been tested, and officially become a Technical College student in a single appointment. It was a slam dunk.

Now, we had only to hold Jason's hand until he completed his federal financial aid paperwork and showed up for the first day of classes. These were critical goalposts for both Jason and my employer. The Technical College didn't get paid unless Jason completed his financial aid paperwork, and the first installment check from the government on Jason's behalf was contingent on his showing up the first week of class. The enrollment staff was held accountable for the new students' showing up on the very first day so as to maximize our "tuition guaranteed" numbers.

At Jason's appointment with financial aid, he learned that after all his aid was applied he would have a tuition balance. The financial aid counselor gave him the standard options. He could make a payment plan. This was something like $400 or so a month, the equivalent of a car loan for a young couple that shared one truck. Needless to say, Jason and Bree could not afford the monthly bill.

Frankly, the financial aid representative did not push the payment plan. That was deliberate. The Technical College wasn't fond of payment-plan students, because the staff had to spend valuable time chasing down those monthly payments. Plus, it was rumored that payment-plan students almost never showed up on the all-important first day of class. I don't have data on that or a clear-cut reason for why it might be true. But, for a whole host of reasons, it isn't hard to imagine that students who are likely to choose a for-profit college don't have significant cash on hand. If they do, their lives are likely to present good reasons to spend that money on something else: food, rent, repairs. As any salesperson or behavioral economist can tell you, every point at which someone exchanges money for a good or service is a moment for them to reconsider their commitment to that purchase. The down payment on that payment plan may be one too many decision points for the likely students at for-profit colleges. Regardless, Jason didn't have the money, the financial aid representative was glad, and off we went to the other options.

Jason could have a family member co-sign for an additional loan. He did not think anyone in his family, except for an aunt, would qualify. Unlike his student loan, the loan his aunt would be taking on had underwriting criteria. The aunt was elderly. She had good credit but was on Social Security. Jason and Bree worried that a loan payment would be too much stress for her. I thought the same thing about Jason and Bree. Sitting in on their financial aid appointments, I increasingly worried that Jason and Bree could not afford the tuition or the risk of the bachelor's degree program he was signing up for. But I was not there to counsel them on their best options. I was there to close.[3] Jason and Bree were prayerful. Consequently, they wouldn't sign on to any of the options without a word from God. That meant they'd leave every appointment with nothing signed, but committed enough to make yet another financial aid appointment.

As the next start date loomed closer and Jason's financial aid package was still not finished, my supervisor, Lisa, pressured me to tell Jason to do what he had to do to make a better life. She pulled me into her office and fired off a set of questions. Had I called the aunt? Did I make Jason bring his aunt's Social Security number? Did I explain to Jason that if he doesn't start he'll never get his life on track? Dissatisfied with my answers—no, I hadn't called his aunt; no, I didn't ask for his aunt's Social Security number; and, no, I didn't tell Jason he was a loser—Lisa erased Jason's tick mark beside my name on the office sales board. She threw open her office door and gathered the entire staff around her. I would be an example: we closed leads, but unless the federal financial aid paperwork and loan agreements were signed off on to satisfy all the tuition, we would all be out of a job soon. She held an impromptu mock session for the whole staff to guide us in reminding those prospects who were dragging their feet that they had told us they wanted better for themselves. It was time to put up or shut up to prove that they really wanted this. To the enrollment staff she said, "I don't know about you, but I own stock. I need people working in this economy so my stocks do well and welfare doesn't drag down the economy." Closing helps the economy.

Whether you are a kindergarten teacher, an admissions counselor, or a college professor, working in education is a lot like being a priest. You shepherd people's collective faith in themselves and their trust in social institutions. When you are a recruiter at a for-profit college, you're more like a television evangelist. The faith sounds alike. The dreams are similar. But instead of big tent revivals that promise strength during difficult times, you sell prayer cloths that promise to solve all of a believer's problems. Today, as a college professor at a "real" university, most people would agree that I'm more priest than televangelist. At least, the world responds to my status—a tenure-track professor and sociologist with a PhD employed at a research university—in a way that says, for all the doubts about the present value of higher education, I am one of the good guys. But, in a previous life, I enrolled Jason in a college considered by many to not be real. Whether I am priest or charlatan depends a great deal on one's belief in education, an article of faith that would distinguish those roles one from another.

As a priest in the educational faith, I can tell you that no matter what Lisa's questionable applied economic theory said, Jason wasn't the economy. Jason was a good kid who had text anxiety and no family wealth to buy test prep, tutors, or anxiety medication. And without the good credit born of wealth, young Jason couldn't make the financial commitment he had to make in order for me to close. I wanted to help Jason, but the Technical College didn't allow us to be priests, only televangelists. We sold, we didn't counsel. We pushed the prayer cloth because a collection plate left too much profit to chance.

One day I turned to a colleague to try to make sense of how I felt. Wasn't I helping Jason change his life for the better? Michael was the most senior enrollment officer in the office. He had worked his way up to only conducting tours of area high school career fairs.[4] He was spared the conversion statistics that ruled the rest of us, confined to the campus backroom where we shared office space. The rumor was that Michael was the only person who our supervisor, Lisa, was too afraid to "coach." That could have been because he was a military veteran, which showed in ways both big and small. While the other enrollment officers' desks were always littered with leads and files stuffed with enrollment paperwork, Michael's desk had the minimalist order of someone who had once made hospital corners on a bed for the sake of national security. It was intimidating.

Michael also had two children preparing for college. One of our employee benefits allowed family members to take courses at the Technical College at a discount. Another colleague, Mary, had taken the job precisely so that her husband could earn a degree on the benefit and quit his job as a plumber. I asked Michael if he was encouraging his eldest son to do the same. He glanced away and said that, while he had thought about it, he had worked hard so that his son had better options. Michael wouldn't stand in his son's way if his son wanted it, but enrolling in the Technical College was not the family plan.

For the first time, I thought carefully about the differences in how our scheduling team sent us prospective leads when they showed up for a campus tour. Prospects who arrived with their parents were moved along quickly, handed a brochure and told to call us if they had any questions. I watched a senior recruiter pull a catalog from the office supply closet when the scheduler told her there were parents out front. Later, I asked her why, and for good reason: we had been trained that catalogs were a last resort. If someone on the phone asked you to mail them information, you were to push for a campus tour, because "it really is best that you see it for yourself." If a prospect came for a tour, the catalog was always the last thing you gave them, after building rapport and prying for their motivations.[5] Catalogs weren't just expensive, they were distant. There was no one like me standing there when you read the catalog, reminding you of your motivations or how easy it is to enroll. Catalogs gave more than we got in return for giving them. In response to my inquiry, the colleague whispered, "He brought his dad" and rolled her eyes as she slipped a business card into the catalog. That family was in and out of the campus tour in less than 15 minutes when tours averaged, in my experience, 30 to 40 minutes. Years later, my research on for-profits found that this was typical. Across nine institutions, the campus tour lasted, on average, 37 minutes.

Not long after my conversation with Michael about the extent to which we were improving lives, the entire office was scheduled for an afternoon meeting with the bigwigs. The Technical College's corporate director was coming to give us a state-of-the-company address. The director had an expensive-looking haircut and a crisp suit. He introduced himself by telling us that he had worked in finance for years and had never before witnessed what was currently happening in the economic markets. It was spring 2008. Access to credit was drying up, including the private student loans on which many of our students relied to cover the gap that Jason was struggling to fill. But, the director said, we shouldn't worry. The company had negotiated a short-term credit solution that would allow us to offer company-backed loans to students like Jason.[6] We should not expect the nosediving market to get in the way of closing.

Three years later, I would be in a sociology PhD program at Emory University. I would have a few economics courses under my belt, new analytical skills, budding research chops, and access to more information than I could have previously imagined. I would better understand what the executive from corporate was telling us that day. I would know that markets were contracting because the precursor to the mortgage crisis that ground the global economy to a halt in the fall of 2008 was beginning to show signs of what would come. As a budding sociologist, I would learn more about the structural dimensions of class and gender and race that made the students at the for-profit cosmetology school where I first worked qualitatively different from the students like Jason whom I enrolled at the Technical College. I would understand the parents who refused to co-sign student loans because, while they believed in education, they were leery of financial contracts that to them looked like payday loans instead of investment portfolios.

I would also come to understand why the short-term loans the executive told me about that day, the ones that set off all my alarm bells and motivated me to quit, would one day be the subject of a federal investigation. The *New York Times* described how ITT Technical Institute (not to be confused with the Technical College) had guaranteed the debt taken on by a private student loan lender (PEAKS). Students who owed more than they could borrow were referred to PEAKS, often without knowing that ITT had a financial stake in PEAKS.[7] Many of these students did not know the terms of private student loans. Those terms, unlike those for federal student loans, have fewer contingencies for repayment and are more expensive when it comes to interest and defaults. The *Times* noted, "Because the lender was unaffiliated with ITT, the loans qualified as private money under the 90-10 rule.[8] The company, therefore, ensured that its students could keep tapping into federal grants for the other 90 percent of their education costs." Evidence suggests that enrollment officers, like me, had no incentive to explain these loans to students—even when they were the only way to close with someone like Jason. The Technical College had no practical way to make good on those loans when students like Jason inevitably couldn't pay them. And, it's worth noting that, in the case of ITT Tech, real violation wasn't in offering these loans to students, but rather in misrepresenting them to investors. We are fine with caveat emptor ("buyer beware") for students, but not for investors. It is a theme that plagues corporate higher education.

Years later, I would also realize how Jason could think that the Technical College was God's will, as education gospels converge with our articles of faith in individual work ethic, self-sacrifice, and gendered norms about being the head of a household. A college education, whether it is a night class in auto mechanics or a graduate degree in physics, has become an individual good. This is in contrast to the way we once thought of higher (or post-secondary) education as a collective good, one that benefits society when people have the opportunity to develop their highest abilities through formal learning. Despite our shift to understanding higher education as a personal good, we have held on to the narrative of all education being inherently good and moral. Economists W. Norton Grubb and Marvin Lazerson call this the education gospel: our faith in education as moral, personally edifying, collectively beneficial, and a worthwhile investment no matter the cost, either individual or societal. Grubb and Lazerson aren't the only ones to allude to education as a faith-based institution. All institutions require our collective faith in them for them to work. We call that legitimacy. But I like Grubb and Lazerson's construction of the education gospel, in part because it speaks to the contradictions in that faith. The gospel was critical to higher education's shift to its vocational promise. That is, the idea that higher education is a moral good is allowable only insofar as higher education serves market interests. Education is good because a good job is good. The faith breaks down when we divorce higher education from jobs. The contradiction is that we don't like to talk about higher education in term of jobs, but rather in terms of citizenship and the public good, even when that isn't the basis of our faith.

Based on the education gospel, we increasingly demand more personal sacrifice from those who would pursue higher education: more loans, fewer grants; more choices, fewer practical options; more possibilities, more risk of failing to attain any of them. We justify that demand by pointing to the significant return in higher wages that those with higher education credentials enjoy. And we imply that this wage premium will continue in the "knowledge economy," where twenty-first-century jobs will require everyone to have some post-secondary education to do highly cognitive work. The gap between the education gospel and the real options available to people—those who need a priest but who instead get a televangelist—is how we end up with *Lower Ed*.

Lower Ed refers to credential expansion created by structural changes in how we work, unequal group access to favorable higher education schemes, and the risk shift of job training, from states and companies to individuals and families, exclusively for profit. Lower Ed is the subsector of high-risk post-secondary schools and colleges that are part of the same system as the most elite institutions. In fact, Lower Ed can exist precisely because elite Higher Ed does. The latter legitimizes the education gospel while the former absorbs all manner of vulnerable groups who believe in it: single mothers, downsized workers, veterans, people of color, and people transitioning from welfare to work. Lower Ed is, first and foremost, a set of institutions organized to commodify social inequalities (see Chapters 3 and 4) and make no social contributions beyond the assumed indirect effect of greater individual human capital. But Lower Ed is not just a collection of schools or set of institutional practices like profit taking and credential granting. Lower Ed encompasses all credential expansion that leverages our faith in education without challenging its market imperatives and that preserves the status quo of race, class, and gender inequalities in education and work. When we offer more credentials in lieu of a stronger social contract, it is Lower Ed. When we ask for social insurance and get workforce training, it is Lower Ed. When we ask for justice and get "opportunity," it is Lower Ed.

Lower Ed is for people like Jason, a fact that wasn't lost on my colleagues at the Technical College. That fact isn't hard to excavate from our social policy and public discussions about for-profit colleges. I have yet to meet a single person who champions for-profit colleges as efficient, individual goods who would also send their own child or relative to a for-profit college. Not even the students I interviewed for this book were willing to agree that they hope their children will attend their alma mater. In subsequent chapters, I will give an example of how social policy, like the workforce-training provisions found in 1996 reforms to welfare, exemplify how our political choices constructed Lower Ed as a legitimate way to navigate the vicissitudes of the labor market. I will show how even critical assessments of for-profit colleges' excesses (or abuses, depending on one's view) make self-evident claims that reinforce the market ethos of Lower Ed. The specific conditions of the new economy make Lower Ed a political choice that more of us will have to reckon with as how we work continues to change (see Chapters 5 and 6). In these ways, we are all complicit in, and victims of, the troubling rise of for-profit colleges in the new economy.

The new economy makes one overriding demand of education: constantly and consistently retrain millions of workers, quickly and at little to no expense for the employer. The new economy is marked by four characteristic changes to the relationships that underpin our social contract: people are frequently changing jobs and employers over their working lifetimes (job mobility); firms place greater reliance on contract, term, and temporary labor (labor flexibility); there is less reliance on employers for income growth and career progression (declining internal labor markets); and workers are shouldering more responsibility for their job training, healthcare, and retirement (risk shift).

In the mad rush for investment capital to consolidate and expand, shareholder for-profit colleges summed up the new economy as "extremely favorable for firms like ours."[9] For-profit colleges promulgated a narrative counter to the one that says eroding job conditions are evidence of the failure of higher education. Instead, for-profit colleges argued to regulators and investors that eroding job conditions were profitable for higher education. Take, for example, Strayer College's investment prospectus in 1998, which described declining federal investment in the military (a significant public employer) and competition for fewer high-quality jobs as "financially beneficial."[10] The conditions were so beneficial that none of the nine shareholder for-profit colleges I applied to considered each other to be major competition for prospective students ("to a far lesser extent other proprietary career colleges," as ITT Tech described its market competitors).[11] Instead, the real competition for prospective students could be found among the employers themselves. "Declining unemployment and underemployment in the labor market and military expansion" could "change projected enrollment viability," said Corinthian Colleges.[12] These shareholder for-profit colleges are the institutions whose tuition rates appear to be pegged to maximum student loan limits, arguably to extract as much profit from students who can borrow the most because they have the least amount of assets and the fewest college choices.

On this point, for-profit colleges are unique among higher education institutions. Traditional colleges were built with the assumption that the social contract of a good job equates to the labor market's rewarding degrees with pay, status, and stability. Even community colleges' original mission was to prepare workers for labor market changes that presumed employers would make a long-term investment in workers. This assumption is still evident in how traditional higher education, from the elites to the open access institutions, understands its relationship to the economy. Most are set up to offer the minimum number of credentials necessary for students to exit the higher education system and not return. It's one reason traditional institutions are slow to change organizationally to accommodate students who do not fit that mold, like working parents. All arguments about how counterproductive that is aside, the fact is that traditional institutions understand the labor market as a partner in absorbing job-training demand from nontraditional student groups. Historically, that has been true with few exceptions. Traditional colleges are (perhaps foolishly) holding out for a return to the social contract of labor market stability and corporate co-investment. Only for-profit colleges in this era of Wall Street investment read the conditions of the new economy as being profitable because of and not *despite* labor market failures—failures they could easily predict would affect millions of workers across traditional divides like "white collar" and "blue collar." In this narrative, the new economy's job crisis produced the behemoth for-profit college crisis of debt, constrained choices, and poor labor market returns—not the other way around.

The new economy is an important part of Jason's story, my story, and the millions of stories bound up in the rapid expansion and specific character of for-profit colleges at the turn of the twenty-first century. As I note in Chapter 2, for-profit colleges are hundreds of years old, but the recent expansion of these profit-generating, credential-granting institutions is different because of *how* they expanded. The largest and most notable of these schools became so incredibly large in the early 2000s by becoming shareholder organizations. Like mortgages that were securitized and traded on Wall Street, financialization shaped the size and logic of the rise of for-profit colleges. These shareholder for-profit colleges told regulators and investors that they were good investment vehicles for three reasons:

- More Americans were graduating from high school, qualifying them for the most basic college admission criteria. But not all high school graduates were graduating from high schools that prepared them for competitive college admissions. Unequal K–12 schools created a market of college-going students while simultaneously creating inequalities among students' abilities to meet admissions criteria.
- Reductions in the U.S. military meant less competition for people who wanted and needed career training but could not or preferred not to go to college.
- Employers were no longer likely to invest in expensive, time-consuming, on-the-job training programs that provided entry-level support or training for career promotion.

Yale political scientist Jacob S. Hacker says the new economy marks both an economic change and an ideological change, each characterized by the "great risk shift" of corporate responsibility to workers and families. Hacker's argument is that incomes have become spikier—they go up and down as workers experience job losses and more frequent changes in their job arrangements. At the same time, workers are expected to plan and invest for their own retirements (401ks and Individual Retirement Accounts), healthcare costs (e.g., Healthcare Savings Accounts), and periods of unemployment (e.g., savings). This risk shift has created an ascendant new work contract that provides fewer buffers to help workers navigate life shocks.

The new economy's work contract affects all workers, albeit differently due to job polarization. That's the phenomenon of highly educated workers pulling ahead financially and socially with near-exclusive access to a shrinking pool of good jobs while less-educated workers are concentrated in on-demand, low-wage jobs with little job security and few promotion ladders. Risk shift for those with good jobs means greater competition for less stability but still high status. Risk shift for those with bad jobs means more of the same poor labor market outcomes and fewer ways to work one's way into a good job.

Hacker identifies two major areas where American workers feel these effects: healthcare and retirement. He calls the shift from corporate responsibility for workers through pensions and health insurance to personal responsibility "risky healthcare" and "risky retirement." To that I would add, "risky credentialing," or Lower Ed. Declining investment in social insurance programs that, by design, diffused the individual risk of old age or health episodes exacerbates the risks associated with sickness and old age. In the same way, declining investment in public higher education exacerbates the risks associated with labor market shocks. As social insurance policies like healthcare and pensions declined, so too did public investment in higher education. Traditional colleges shifted more of the cost of a credential (or risk) to students and families with more loans and fewer grants offered, even as steep price discounting fought to hold individual costs down. The U.S. Federal Reserve explains that "the decline in state government support and increasing generosity of financial aid are both aspects of a broader paradigm shift from broad, publicly-subsidized higher education to greater reliance on tuition payments from students and their families." [13] This pattern is true for all of higher education, but it is most true, in the extreme, at for-profit colleges that are by definition tuition dependent.

Despite the inevitableness of the rhetoric about how for-profit colleges serve a necessary market function, it did not have to be this way. The decision to encourage or allow expansion to happen in the private sector instead of in the public sector was a political choice to uphold neoliberal ideas of individualism, markets, and profit taking. Even when we deigned to offer new schemes to offset the cost of higher education we came up with individual education savings accounts, when fifty years ago we may have massively expanded federal grant programs, work training grants, or public-sector employment.[14] The shareholder for-profit colleges that were responsible for the majority of the growth in the sector during its most profitable era said in their regulatory findings that this ideology, above all, guaranteed them access to federal student aid programs and relatively little competition for the millions of workers who had few options if they wanted a good job. And, should for-profit degrees not lead to a good job, our ideology of personal responsibility absolves the institutions. Essentially, we believe that Jason should have known better.

When I think back on my interactions with Jason, I always remember Michael as well, who explained to me in his own way how Lower Ed remains a stable part of our higher education system. With a sigh, Michael told me that free tuition at the Technical College was still not quite cheap enough to offset the risk of sending his African American, middle-class son to a college that he marketed almost daily to high school students across the state. I wish I had asked that executive speaking to our staff where he earned his own degrees in finance.[15] I wish I had asked more questions about the terms of those school-backed loans. I wish I had done many things that I did not do because, not unlike the students I cold-called from that long desk, I did not know how to talk about school as anything but the savior of those seeking salvation.

Instead of asking all the right questions when the corporate director showed up, I went home that day and did some prayerful meditation of my own. I called my alma mater, a "real" school, a historically black school, and asked if I could come back. The registrar put me on hold. And when she returned, I was enrolled. The next day I left a resignation notice on my corner of the long table at the Technical College. But before I got in my Jetta to head

down a path of unraveling my experiences in the for-profit college
sector, I walked to the bathroom and called Jason from my cellphone. I left a voicemail urging him to call the counselor at the
local community college. I don't know whether he got the message
and heeded my advice, or if he ended up finding a way to pay the
tuition difference at the Technical College. But the more I learned
about the conflict between the education gospel and how we do
credentialing in the new economy, the more I hoped Jason never
showed up for a $72,000 bachelor's degree in electrical engineer-
ing technology at the Technical College.

Getting to the Gospel

The for-profit college landscape is specific, complex, and in a moment of rapid change. Depending on who you are, ads for these
schools started exploding across your television, radio, and newspapers about eight years ago. That's when the formerly "sleepy
sector" of private, profit-generating colleges made a demonstrable
jump from advertising during late night infomercials and daytime
judge shows to targeting middle America during primetime.[16] If
you think of bucolic college campuses and glossy folders when you
think about college information, then the for-profit college ads
you saw were bombastic. If you don't think of much at all when
you think about college, then the ads were likely less bombastic
and probably more successful. Either way, these ads marked an era
of higher education in the United States that was unique for its
scale, scope, and structure.

   For-profit colleges have been with us for at least two hundred years, but large, national (and increasingly multinational)
for-profit colleges are a beast particular to the current moment.
These institutions have names that conjure vague images of aspira-
tion without any concrete link to people or histories; names like
Strayer and Argosy and, of course, the University of Phoenix. The

names, or brands, can now be found on football stadiums, on the backs of sponsored Olympic athletes, and as sponsored content in mainstream magazines. Increasingly, for-profit college leaders can be found sharing space with U.S. presidents (and presidential hopefuls),[17] the technology sector elite, and some of the most powerful boards in corporate America. In that way, these schools are not dissimilar to Harvard, Yale, and Princeton for the company they keep and the powerful connections they boast. But, whereas the most elite "traditional" (or, not-for-profit) colleges can be said to derive their cachet from the cachet of their students, for-profit colleges cannot. The social distance between the president of the University of Phoenix (who earned almost $5 million in salary in 2013) and the typical University of Phoenix student is far greater than the distance between the president of Harvard ($900,000 in salary in 2013) and the typical Harvard student (well, the student's family). The intersections of power and poverty, extreme wealth creation and inequalities that grow more extreme, are right there in the gaps. And those intersections bring about questions: how we got here; where here is, exactly; and, most important, what it all means to the everyday lives of those who are affected most.

By my count of newspaper articles published over the past twenty years, the American public started to take a keen interest in the latest era of for-profit colleges sometime in 2005. That's when you see a discernible and prolonged uptick in stories about the University of Phoenix, Strayer University, and Everest College. These institutions had the financial capital and aggressive growth strategies to flood local radio, television, billboard, and public transit advertising. They implored you to call today and start tomorrow for a better job in computer technology, healthcare, and business. And those ads worked. They worked very well. By 2014, the sector of profit-generating colleges that I will call "for-profit" throughout this book had increased its aggregate enrollment since 1998 by 225 percent to 2.1 million students, according to the National Center for Education Statistics.

There are a few ways to think about those millions of students. In one narrative, a couple of million people all woke up one day and decided to go to college. They did so for different individual reasons that are too complicated to be ascertained, but that are generally related to the "skillification" of the U.S. economy.[18] In another narrative, decades of deregulation culture opened the federal student aid tap to predatory for-profit degree shills who would enroll anyone with a pulse to get their hands on sweet, sweet, publicly subsidized, government-guaranteed cash. Both narratives bring to light different aspects of a historically distinct era of credentialing in the United States. For the first time, the expansion of mass U.S. higher education did not happen in the not-for-profit or state sectors but rather in the financialized sector. That means these institutions weren't founded by churches or state governments. And, unlike earlier iterations of for-profit colleges, these institutions weren't started and owned by private owners. These were college brands owned by shareholders for whom the credential was a means to profit as opposed to an end. These shares could be bought and traded. These transactions created (for all involved) a fundamentally different relationship to tuition, revenue, and profit. Financialized entities are generally concerned with growth rather than stability, necessitating quarter-over-quarter increases in revenue. In an industry where 90 percent of revenues are generated from enrollment, that means financialized institutions are concerned first and foremost with enrollment growth.[19] If budgets are moral documents, the fact that some financialized for-profit colleges reportedly spent 22.4 percent of all revenue on marketing, advertising, recruiting, and admissions staffing compared with 17.7 percent of all revenue, on instruction speaks to the morals of financialization.[20]

The dueling narratives over why and how these financialized shareholder for-profit colleges happened are important, but they do not go so far as to ask *to what end did financialized higher education expand?* I think about the question of "to what end" a lot. I think about that question because it is the way to think about how higher education is not an island unto itself but is instead a crucial, interrelated system of people, ideas, and degrees embedded in our greater social fabric. Higher education is linked to everything from our slaveholding histories to our imagined technocratic futures. At heart, higher education is a means both of redressing socioeconomic inequality and of perpetuating socioeconomic inequalities in new guises. For these reasons, the expansion of for-profit colleges is about more than just a set of schools that generate income from tuition for distribution to owners and investors. For-profit colleges are a way to understand the ultimate ends of most social inquiry: how does this change who and what we are? That means thinking about the ways in which the expansion of financialized higher education—of which for-profit colleges are the exemplar—capture, commodify, and entrench social inequalities.

I make an explicit claim in this book: for-profit colleges are distinct from traditional not-for-profit colleges in that their long-term viability depends upon acute, sustained socioeconomic inequalities. All of higher education benefits from inequality in some way, but only for-profit colleges exclusively, by definition, rely on persistent inequalities as a business model.[21] They do this in numerous ways. By their own description across various official documents, for-profit colleges rely on prospective students whose aspirations outstrip their available options for mobility. Further, these prospective students are considered a valuable asset only insofar as our social conditions keep producing them. Our current system of unequal K–12 schools, the prestige-driven hierarchy of traditional higher education, need-based student aid financing, and declining labor market security are continually producing aspirations that aren't viable by any other means except by gaining more credentials in perpetuity. More credentials in perpetuity for a population with aspirations but limited means of mobility is a bad social prescription for a healthy body politic, but it is a very profitable prescription for Lower Ed. In their modern iteration, for-profit colleges have distributed risk through shareholder organizations, achieved significant scale to manage profits, and captured student populations that are very sensitive to macroeconomic changes in work. While some corporate brands have caved trying to balance the needs of those populations with their shareholder structure, many others remain in business. They may change in scale (and data available at the time of this writing suggest that this is already under way), but for-profit colleges are unlikely to die out as long as the conditions that produced them remain. Indeed, if all for-profit colleges were to go out of business tomorrow, workers would still desire the economic security and mobility that credentials promise. We would still have a financing scheme that makes poverty profitable. Some other Lower Ed credentialing scheme would simply fill the void.

To better understand that void and how people are experiencing it, in this book I take up the task of moving beyond what for-profit colleges *are* to understand *why* they are and what that means for the public and its institutions. There are a few things you should know about how I do that. I draw on my experiences in for-profit colleges as well as my academic study of them. My experiences in the for-profit sector are invaluable. I saw firsthand the gaps between procedure and reality in marketing, enrollment, recruiting, and the classroom. I worked at two opposite ends of the for-profit college spectrum: a certificate-granting cosmetology-career school chain and a large national shareholder college that offered associate's, bachelor's, and graduate degrees. I have exhausted all possible avenues to account for the limits of memory. For six years I kept an online journal on a website called LiveJournal.com. I kept that journal during my tenure at both for-profit colleges. I have long since stopped keeping that journal, but I made an archive of everything I wrote over six years for posterity. I found that file when I started thinking about this book and was surprised by how often I documented my workday, as well as my thoughts and feelings about that work. I have used that to augment my memory. I also sent many emails to friends about that work during that time. Fortunately, I never subscribed to the "inbox zero" craze. I had many of those emails saved and I hounded friends to search their inboxes as well. These archives inform my memory of events, but this book draws on more than my experiences.

In 2010, I started a PhD program at Emory University intending to study anything but for-profit colleges. Fortunately, a mentor pushed the issue when he learned about my experience. He argued that my experience would only sharpen the training I was receiving as a social scientist and would bring to bear a multi-faceted, nuanced read of a complex social phenomenon. I resisted for about a year but eventually conceded to his wisdom. The questions I developed took on a new urgency with every exchange, and I had many exchanges with students at for-profit colleges who— through friends and relations—sought me out to ask for help. The urgency increased as I talked with traditional academics who were fascinated by the problem of for-profit colleges but who were detached from the people in them. The urgency really amped up when I finally understood that all roads of inequality—families, schools, income, wealth, class, gender, and race—ran through the conundrum of popular, beleaguered, high-cost, for-profit colleges.

By 2011, I had embarked upon a doctoral dissertation that, in formal terms, was a political economy of market-based credential expansion in the United States during the Wall Street era of for-profit colleges. In laymen's terms, I spent five years trying to determine what produced the rapid financialization and growth of for-profit colleges. With support from the American Educational Research Association's Research Conference Grant and my colleagues at Duke University's Research Network on Racial and Ethnic Inequality, I convened an academic conference on for-profit colleges in 2011. In addition to researchers, senior executives from four for-profit colleges joined the two-day conference. I also interviewed 109 students formerly or currently enrolled in for-profit colleges at every level of the sector, from students in mechanical certificate programs to students in psychology PhD programs. I recruited most students by standing outside buildings located in what I call a for-profit college triangle: an area in a suburb of Atlanta, Georgia, where a train line had a single stop boasting three for-profit colleges at one intersection. I also recruited students online and through referrals. I met with students face to face whenever possible and also conducted interviews via Skype and telephone. I discuss my methods further in the appendix.

From those students, I got a sense of the context of their educational choices and I learned fairly quickly that their context was always about more than just education. Their experiences led me to consider how the for-profit college apparatus perfectly suited the complex contexts of so many students' lives given that those students are different in so many ways. To understand that apparatus, I enrolled in nine shareholder for-profit college brands in Atlanta, Georgia, over the course of a year starting in 2012. Enrolling meant going from first point of contact—"call today!"—to the first opportunity to sign an enrollment agreement at each of the colleges. My enrollment exercise included phone calls, email exchanges, and on-campus interviews. That fieldwork drove home how remarkably similar for-profit colleges are to each other and why that similarity is so efficient for so many different student populations. The efficiency works because more and more people are similarly affected by changes in how we work in the new economy. The risk for changing jobs and moving up the professional ladder has shifted to individual workers across race, class, and gender. That risk makes credentials valuable only insofar as those credentials are easy to start, easy to fit into complex lives, and easy to pay for. For-profit colleges nail that trifecta for millions of people who are similarly vulnerable in this new economy of risk shift, declining job tenure, and insecurity.

In Chapter 4, I share data from interviews with students, all women, who formed an online support group. These women were enrolled in upmarket degree programs at for-profit colleges—the bachelor's, master's, and doctoral degrees that also distinguish this era of for-profit college expansion from previous ones. These degrees are the most expensive and the most risky. These students refute the argument that people in for-profit colleges are low-information consumers. All of these students had bachelor's degrees. Most of them had experience in traditional higher education. They knew how to do "real" college. How they make sense of their degrees, educational choices, and futures with a for-profit college credential is important. They demonstrate that the contradictions of the education gospel in many ways legitimize for-profit colleges for students, if not for employers.

Throughout the book, I anonymize interviewees, students, and some biographical details if they are not important to the analysis. My autobiographical details are not anonymized, as I own that story. I lived in Charlotte, North Carolina. I worked for a cosmetology school and a vocational school in the early 2000s. I quit my job in the way that I described. I attended graduate school. I earned my PhD in sociology and am a professor at Virginia Commonwealth University. Some student profiles presented are composites, but all quoted dialogue is attributed to a single respondent. I also anonymize the names of executives from the for-profit colleges. I interviewed eleven presidents, directors, and other corporate-level for-profit college actors over the course of my research. I anonymize them because the individuation of for-profit colleges is mostly a distraction. Whether someone at a for-profit college misleads a student or preys on poor people is really irrelevant to my argument, although it may be interesting. As a sociologist, my faith is in structures and institutions—things that are bigger than individuals and that would hum along even if the people in them weren't minding the store. Fundamentally, institutions that can turn inequality into profit even when we, citizens and persons, would agree that it is immoral for them to do so provide a far more interesting and powerful account than the impact of any single actor. This, I conclude, is the case with the troubling rise of Lower Ed.

My conclusions are all old news to for-profit colleges according to their own institutional narratives, which I have pieced together through financial documents. I have analyzed the paperwork that publicly traded for-profit colleges filed with the Securities and Exchange Commission between 1992 and 2013. I have analyzed the educational biographies of for-profit college presidents and conducted quantitative and qualitative analyses of financial newspapers' coverage of the sector during its boom years. Some of that work can be read in scholarly books, academic journals, and in various media stories I have written over the years. More personally, I have advised students and parents who email me, concerned that they have chosen poorly. I have engaged the many students who write to me angry that no one understands how hard he or she worked for their degree at a for-profit college. In these pages, I merge experience with empirics. It is an account of why for-profit colleges are not only here, and here in a big way, but also why they are likely to stay here given our social and economic conditions. I write as a sociologist and as a human, because these data and this phenomenon deserve nothing less.

1

THE REAL

The questions surrounding for-profit higher education are endless. Are they real schools? Do their students get jobs? Do they prey on poor and minority students? Are they ripping off the taxpayer? Are they a beacon of hope for students whom traditional higher education cannot or will not serve? Let's take these questions in turn and then move on to what they *don't* quite tell us.

First, for-profit colleges are real in the sense that you can see them and touch them. If they offer federal student aid, they are also accredited. The Department of Education (ED) has a list of approved accreditors, the official gatekeepers that determine which institutions can participate in the program. Accreditation is expensive to acquire and was originally designed for the needs of traditional post-secondary institutions. That is why some accreditation agencies, for example the Southern Accreditation Council of Schools (SACS), assess infrastructure holdings like the number of volumes in the library. For-profit colleges keep operating expenses low to maximize their profit margins on the revenue generated from student tuition. Investing in and holding 20,000 books would take a serious bite out of that profit margin. Beginning in the 1980s, for-profit colleges organized to lobby for different and more lenient accreditation standards. National agencies (as opposed to regional accreditors like SACS) emerged as a response.[1] Accreditation had been a long-standing gentlemen's agreement among similarly prestigious institutions. With challenges from for-profit colleges, critics are increasingly questioning accreditors' ability to monitor the quality of a sprawling, diverse field of schools.

Do students from for-profits get jobs? These data are still being debated.[2] The most recent research finds that for-profit colleges do a better job than community colleges of getting poor and minority students to complete short-term certificates, and about as fair if slightly worse than community colleges with associate's degree completions. Should students complete their course of study, one experimental study found that students with for-profit college credentials on their resume or application are as likely to get a callback as someone with only a high school diploma.[3] Another study found that applicants with a for-profit college credential get as many callbacks as applicants with a fake college listed. This means that employers may have a preference for traditional degrees, but they lack the mechanisms to discern which schools confer them beyond the big state and brand-name schools. Thus, when applicants lack a credential from a popular or well-known traditional institution, they may as well not have one at all when it comes to expecting a callback. For-profit college students earn about as much as graduates of similar demographic backgrounds from traditional colleges, but have more bouts of unemployment and for longer periods of time. All of this information, it should be noted, is severely constrained by various institutional policies that make it difficult to track individual earnings across educational careers and the labor market.

Do for-profit colleges prey on poor and minority students? NPR's Tony Cox asked the then president of the industry's professional organization, Harris Miller, precisely that.[4] At the time, the group was called Career Colleges of America. It was 2007, and after a decade of rapid growth fueled by advertisements designed to "create demand," it was hard to ignore how many of those ads featured African Americans. Cox asked Miller, "Do you target African-Americans through your commercials and other recruitment efforts?" Miller responded with an emphatic "no" and went on to say that they target anyone trying "to get ahead." At the same time, Miller touts the sector's high African American enrollment, comparing it specifically to the University of Virginia and UCLA, as evidence that for-profit colleges are a force for democratic college access. The sector not only maintains that line, but charges traditional colleges with elitism for refusing to compete for the students who enroll in for-profit colleges. What is clear is that poor and minority students are disproportionately enrolled in for-profit colleges. "[For-profit college students] are more likely to be female and much more likely to be non-White [than students enrolled in traditional colleges]. They are also less likely to be single, but more likely to have a dependent and be single parents."[5] Given the median wealth position of African Americans ($719), Hispanics ($1,296), and the poor (who by definition have negligible wealth positions), the high tuition price of for-profit colleges and their unimpressive labor market returns call into question the concept of "preying," if a rose by any other name is still a rose. It is effect, not intent, that matters.

The most common questions about for-profits boil down to two: are for-profit colleges legitimate, "real" colleges, and does their growth mean greater access or greater insecurity? Since the sector's impressive era of enrollment growth kicked off in the mid-1990s, researchers have primarily concerned themselves with the kinds of questions we are trained to ask. We have measured the labor market returns on for-profit degrees. We have measured some demographic characteristics of students in for-profit colleges. And we have measured whether for-profit college students repay their tax-supported student loan debts. Those are questions of *what*: what the students are, what their debt loads are, and what employers think of their degrees. We have not asked as many questions about *why*. In particular, we have not asked why for-profit colleges' exponential growth happened when it did, and precisely who was most affected.[6] (The *how* of it all has not been explored thoroughly either, especially in terms of how for-profit colleges shape the textured, real lives of everyday people—more on this in later chapters.)

For sure, there are theories about this. You get an education researcher and former president of the largest academic organization of education researchers, William Tierney, arguing that for-profit colleges expanded because they offer better customer service and clearer occupational connections than do traditional colleges, which are more concerned with prestige than practical curriculums. A foremost authority on the history of for-profit colleges, Kevin Kinser, argues that the massive Wall Street financialization of shareholder for-profit colleges (like the University of Phoenix and other large brands) provided capital for the for-profit college sector to consolidate and expand. These are useful interpretations, but they are not entirely satisfying. Just because Strayer University can expand does not mean that it will. Data on the labor market's reception of for-profit credentials does not suggest that the sector's practical orientation bears much fruit for graduates. Furthermore, neither of their explanations address the fact that for-profit students are less likely to graduate than are students with similar demographics in traditional higher education. While there is some debate about the extent to which these are apples-to-apples comparisons, even the most generous read of the available data reveals that students in for-profit colleges have more risk factors for dropping out.[7] And when they do, they carry more relative and actual debt than they would have had they been at a less expensive school, which might explain why they account for almost half of all student loan defaults.[8]

The latest research in this area remains primarily interested in how employers view for-profit college credentials and how much for-profit college graduates earn. To revisit a point made previously, recall that employers do not show markedly better reads of the profit status of colleges than do students; however, anecdotal evidence abounds regarding how human resources professionals develop informal screening processes to weed out "diploma mills."

We don't know if a for-profit credential is just a poor status signal for employers or if it is a type of negative credential that marks workers as likely being poor, minority, female, or somehow low status. All of this research focuses on those who actually earn a for-profit credential, while the majority of those who enroll in for-profit colleges do not even graduate. We do not have good data on what happens to them in either education or the labor market. These kinds of data could go a long way toward explaining how for-profit colleges expanded, how new forms of Lower Ed might expand, and the cost of all these credentials in dollars and lives. Taken together, this set of facts signals a need for greater scrutiny than researchers have attempted thus far, and especially for deeper and more sustained qualitative research on the various aspects of how Lower Ed credentials are produced, taken up, and interpreted.[9]

Nevertheless, there is plenty of working knowledge about this sector on which we can begin to build a much fuller picture of why this growth has come to pass. For-profit colleges are profit-seeking entities that produce credentials for the express purpose of generating profit for the colleges' owners. For-profit colleges "use the language of colleges and universities but operate like corporations or sole-proprietorships."[10] For-profit colleges are precisely defined by their tax status, which allows them to generate profit that can be extracted and distributed to shareholders and/or owners. In contrast, traditional not-for-profit colleges can participate in revenue-generating activities (and they do; see: patents and collegiate sports teams), but their tax status dictates how they can extract profit and to what ends. For-profit colleges can extract excess revenue and distribute it as profit, whereas not-for-profit colleges cannot. The "for-profit college" designation has become a discursive distinction that represents differences in prestige (both institutional and among students enrolled), legitimacy, and functional value in the labor market.

Scholars and policymakers have paid greater attention to

for-profit colleges because of their recent rapid growth, and I focus on this time period for the same reasons they do: scale and
form. Two million students were enrolled at for-profit colleges in
2010, up from less than 400,000 in 2000, and that growth was
not evenly distributed.[11] While 1 in 20 of all students in higher
education is enrolled in a for-profit college, 1 in 10 black students,
1 in 14 Latino students, and 1 in 14 first-generation college students is enrolled at a for-profit college. The typical for-profit college student is a woman and a parent. For-profit colleges dominate
in producing black bachelor's degree holders.[12] While there has
been a lot made of the declining enrollments at for-profit colleges
between 2012 and 2015, the fact remains that this is mostly related to rates of growth. Growth has, in fact, been declining during this more recent period. Save a few notable implosions, like the
phased closure and eventual change in ownership of Corinthian-
owned for-profit Everest Colleges in 2015, many for-profit colleges
continue to enroll students, and the overall share of the for-profit
college subsector of higher education is fairly stable. Still, the previous aggregate growth and disproportionate enrollment of un-
derrepresented student groups causes some to argue that for-profit
colleges offer unprecedented access to college, while others argue
that these patterns indicate greater inequality of access to "legitimate" college educations.

For-profit colleges are often cited as offering occupational
training that traditional colleges and universities do not offer.
Researchers Guilbert C. Hentschke, Vincente M. Lechuga, and
William G. Tierney repeat a common line that attributes the
growth of for-profits to their career-focused orientation when they
say that for-profits "offer career-oriented programs for which there
are proportionately large numbers of workplace vacancies." [13]
They are not alone. Of the 33 peer-reviewed academic papers
and books about for-profit colleges published between 2000 and
2008, 82 percent of them used some version of this narrative of
for-profit colleges' being more attuned to the labor market by of-

fering career-oriented degrees to justify for-profits' rapid growth
and popularity. There are largely two ways that academics tend to
understand the growth of for-profit colleges. One way says they
grew to meet consumer demand that traditional colleges don't
meet for various reasons (elitism, financial constraints, politics,
and accreditation requirements). Another way to understand this
phenomenon is alternately called *credentialing theory* or *credentialism*. This says that something about the unequal distribution
of jobs and access to those jobs generates demand for degrees or
credentials. We might best understand the rapid growth of a new
kind of college by understanding the current inequalities in access
to (and returns from) traditional higher education. I subscribe to
the latter framework.[14]

For-profit colleges historically offered short-term credentials
and, later, associate's degrees. But the Wall Street era of expansion
(1994 to present) that spurred contemporary debate has seen the
sector expand into offering more bachelor's, graduate, and professional degrees.[15] In 1996, public colleges awarded more than half
of all master's degrees conferred in the United States, and for-
profits conferred too few to be recorded in federal data sets. By
2012, the public college share of conferred master's degrees was 46
percent, while for-profit colleges conferred 10 percent of all master's degrees awarded.[16] The fastest-growing subsector of for-profit
college credential offerings has been in what I call up-market degrees. These are credential sequences that start at a lower level, with
higher degrees stacked on top as demand increases. For example,
in 2001 ITT Technical Institute told investors that "[m]anage-
ment believes that the introduction of higher level programs at additional ITT Technical Institutes will attract more students and
increase the number of students continuing their studies beyond
the associates degree level."[17] The financial motive to keep costs
low while expanding enrollment makes it cost-effective to offer
higher degrees in curriculums the schools already provide. Take,
for instance, Capella University, which specializes in upmarket

credentials. In 2004, they created two new bachelor's degree programs in business administration and information technology.[18] Capella saw its niche as allowing those technology-sector workers with certificates and associate's degrees to apply those credits to a specialty "bachelor's degree completion program" in information technology. These upmarket degree spirals contextualize the fact that fall enrollments in programs lasting four years or more "increased most rapidly in the for-profit sector, 52% between fall 2003 and fall 2006."[19] In 2005–2006, for-profit colleges awarded 3 percent of all doctoral degrees. Three for-profit colleges (Capella, Strayer, and the University of Phoenix) award PhDs in fields as diverse as psychology and education, and for-profit owner Infilaw operates three accredited law schools in Florida, North Carolina, and Arizona.[20]

That's important context to bear in mind, but let's return for a moment to the idea that for-profit colleges, no matter what we think of them, are providing credentials in fields where there are labor market shortages. The first thing we might expect, were that as unilaterally true as is often presented, is that those with for-profit college credentials would see significant returns on their credentials. Again, that evidence is mixed. We should see high rates of employment. Yet the best available data there show that this isn't true of for-profit college graduates. And, considering that the majority of full-time undergraduate students enrolled in a for-profit college will not have graduated after six years, the mixed results we *do* know about graduates don't even apply to most of the students in Lower Ed. It can still be argued that the dropout rates and unemployment rates and low wages are about who the students are: poor, working class, women, and vulnerable with poor job-seeking and work habits with lots of risks for failure, no matter what kind of credential they pursue. One study does find that in some local labor markets for-profit college enrollment is related to employment growth and higher wages in the area.[21] That could mean that people are going to for-profit colleges when their local labor markets change and they need new skills to get the new kinds of jobs. But it does not mean that for-profit college expansion in high-demand occupational areas leads to those jobs. Let's look at an example from healthcare.

Researchers and public policy makers frequently cite healthcare as the occupational category that best justifies the existence and expansion of for-profit colleges. Each of the books and articles exclusively about for-profit colleges that I cite in this chapter, save two, mentions the importance of healthcare to the new economy, the need to train millions of workers for it, and the unique role of for-profit colleges in providing that training. A 2011 report from the Center for American Progress looks at the role of for-profit schools in training the healthcare workforce.[22] The report puts a fine point on a distinction that is important in order to understand the rhetoric of for-profit colleges versus the reality: the occupational category of "healthcare" is very broad and diverse. It includes everything from your primary care physician to the housekeeping workers at the local hospital. We know for-profits don't put any dent at all in credentialing medical doctors, physician's assistants, or dentists—areas that also have critical labor needs. But maybe they do provide the all-important nurses and healthcare technology aides, like radiologists. Yet even there, this report finds, for-profit colleges overstate their case: "for-profit schools are making only modest contributions to training the highest demand health professionals." The report says this is due in part to the difference in specialties that for-profit colleges have curriculums in and those specialties the labor market actually needs. For example, the second most popular "healthcare" certificate program in for-profit colleges is massage therapy. That's not exactly what we think of when we think of critical healthcare needs—and for good reason. The most critical needs areas in healthcare are registered nurses and physicians, especially in elder care due to the aging baby boomer population. Students may like massage therapy. And because for-profits make money when they offer programs that students like, it makes sense to offer more massage therapy programs than our labor market can probably absorb. We can call that healthcare, but the program isn't meeting the critical labor market training needs that the for-profits say they are, or that research assumes they are when broad occupational categories are used to measure these changes.

The Financialized Wall Street Era of For-Profit Colleges and What It Means for Inequality

The majority of for-profit colleges are small, but the most notable ones are the largest, which bear those names we know so well: the University of Phoenix and ITT Technical Institute, to name two. Historically, for-profit colleges have been privately owned, mostly by single proprietors, and often were family-owned local operations. In the 1990s, for-profit colleges' expansion had a particular characteristic. The Wall Street era of for-profit higher education is "marked by the new visibility of publicly owned corporate providers."[23] The current era is "defined by Wall Street institutions."[24] For-profit colleges do not simply participate in revenue-generating activities, as do all institutions of higher education. Instead, for-profit colleges are singularly defined by their profit-seeking imperative.

Randy Martin has called our current socioeconomic culture one where daily life has been financialized.[25] Rather than exchanging money for goods, increasingly consumers use credit and debt to construct their social lives and its accoutrements. At the macro level, markets have financialized mortgages (see: the 2009 housing crisis) and education spending (see: student loans). As it pertains to for-profit colleges, financialization refers to the period in which for-profit credentialing organizations were transformed into "favorable markets" by using growth and acquisition strategies consistent with shareholder business organizations. Those favorable markets are not naturally occurring phenomenon; they come from somewhere. And they are profitable for reasons that suggest the success of for-profit colleges in their current form is a barometer of deep, far-reaching inequalities.

Despite the claims that for-profit colleges serve an unmet need, are more nimble than stodgy traditional colleges, and increase access to poor and minority students, we know that for-profit colleges are related to inequality. We just shroud the inequality in euphemisms that don't challenge the conventional wisdom of the educational gospel. It's there, even in the rosiest interpretations of the rise of for-profit higher education, or Lower Ed, at the turn of the twenty-first century. When economists say that these agile, responsive institutions are better suited to career training, they're talking about inequality. In the knowledge economy, technological advancements make human labor more efficient. We can produce more with fewer workers. A consequence of that efficiency has been greater economic insecurity.[26] The more insecure people feel, the more they are willing to spend money for an insurance policy against low wages, unemployment, and downward mobility. Those least likely to have an insurance policy that our labor market values are people for whom higher education has always been a long shot: poor people, single parents, the socially isolated, African Americans, the working class. When education researchers talk about the unmet consumer demand that for-profit colleges serve, they're talking about inequality. Who is mostly likely to go to good schools with college prep classes and have medical care and stable housing, to focus on standardized tests and have the money to participate in extracurricular activities? And, who does not have those social resources, the social resources that many traditional colleges assume their likely student will have? When investors and politicians say that for-profit colleges offer a flexible solution to retrain our workforce, they are talking about inequality. Whose training in the jobs of the twentieth century is now obsolete in the twenty-first century? Who needs a flexible solution? Women who carry the burden of primary childcare,[27] men working more than one job, older adults caring for both their parents and their own children[28]—a group for whom time isn't just money, but the absence of money.

Flexible solutions, on-demand educations, open access career retraining, reskilling, and upskilling—these are terms that talk about inequality without taking inequality seriously. When we use these words and conceptualizations of for-profit higher education, we end up reaching some strange conclusions. We blame people with "low cognitive abilities" for enrolling in "low quality" for-profit colleges. We argue that more for-profit colleges are a democratic good even when we know that the most vulnerable students pay a high price for attending them. We argue that consumers drive products, as if students are consuming degrees rather than the promise of a good job. In effect, we blame people for doing precisely what the education gospel demands that they do.

From my experience on the ground working in for-profit colleges, and later when studying them, I realized there is a more satisfying if damning explanation for the rise of for-profit colleges in the Wall Street era of Lower Ed. Inequalities in how we work, exacerbated by social policies and legitimized by individualist notions of education as a consumer good, conspired to create the demand for a credential that would insure workers against bad jobs. And everyone from politicians to employers to researchers and those in traditional higher education benefited when for-profit colleges became the solution to that demand. Even the students who succeeded at for-profit colleges paid a price that's not usually associated with the education gospel. Many took on significant debt. Those who took on less thanks to employer tuition plans or veteran's benefits are still part of a system that will likely ask them to get more credentials in the future. They'll re-enter the higher education pipeline with a for-profit degree—a credential that makes it hard to move back into traditional higher education, which may be more prestigious, less expensive, or better suited for the student.[29] And those are the success stories. The more likely story is the student who finishes with high debt or more debt than their salary can absorb—say, a nursing assistant. Or the student who doesn't finish, perhaps the most vulnerable of all students. They have debt, no degree, and all the burdens that made them likely to attend a for-profit college in the first place. For these students, the problem of inequalities in access and outcomes is clearly a consequence of Lower Ed's expansion.

But there's a larger story of inequality, one that affects all of us. It's the story about whether we can afford to subsidize Lower Ed at its current scale as anti-poverty programs and social welfare safety nets continue to shrink or become harder to access. It's the story of our willingness to make a high-cost, high-risk, debt-driven system of higher education absorb the demand among workers who—as almost every expert predicts—will increasingly have to go back to college many times to stay employable.[30] That's the challenge for all of higher education, but only in Lower Ed is the challenge singular, especially expensive, and perversely profitable. It's the story of Lower Ed's retraining workers, at the individuals' expense, subsidized by taxpayers, for our entire working life course as we live longer, wages stagnate, childcare and healthcare costs continue to rise, and the social safety net frays. The troubling rise of for-profit colleges, despite their boom-and-bust investment cycles, is a symptom of larger issues wrought by changes in how we work and our unwillingness to legislate in order to protect our social contract. In all of us is some part of Jason—his hope, his learning disabilities, his family, his challenges, his faith, his community, his past, and his future.

2

THE BEAUTY COLLEGE AND
THE TECHNICAL COLLEGE

By 2004, the Beauty College had become a national brand. It had three locations in my hometown of Charlotte, North Carolina. I had never heard of the Beauty College until a recruiter emailed me about a job for which my "resume at Monster.com indicated [I] was very qualified." I had been to college but was twenty or so credits shy of a degree. I had corporate training experience at a Fortune 500 telecom. I had writing experience. And I did not have any idea what a for-profit college was. When I showed up to interview for the position of admissions counselor at the Beauty College, I was not very different from the hundreds of students I would eventually enroll in certificate, bachelor's, and graduate degree programs. At the height of the for-profit college sector's rapid expansion in the first decade of the twenty-first century, I worked ground zero at two for-profit colleges for a total (according to the Social Security Administration) of twenty-five months.

These two schools—which I will refer to as the Beauty College and the Technical College—represent the poles of the for-profit college's Wall Street era. As the previous chapter explains in more detail, this period is defined as one when the investment classes not only recognized the huge economic potential of on-demand market-based degrees, but also when millions of people suddenly needed more on-demand education to stay afloat in the labor market. The pull between "good jobs" in information technology and business and "bad jobs" in the service sector shaped the world of life and work by the 2000s. When and how deeply you felt pulled by these magnetic energies depended greatly on things beyond your control: who you were, what you were, what you inherited, what you knew, who you knew, and where you were on the social ladder of opportunity when the poles started pulling apart. The poles of the for-profit college sector reflect that greater push and pull. Short-term certificates with clearly articulated job paths, like nine-month cosmetology degrees at the Beauty College, enroll more brown people, more women, and more poor people. At the other end, master's degrees in technology, like the twenty-four-month programs at the Technical College, enroll more men—a greater share of whom are white, less poor, have some college already, and have more immediate earning power. The student populations look somewhat different, and they seem to have different immediate goals. Yet over the years I have learned just how much they—and I—had in common.

I listened to story after story about what made people call a 1-800 number after an ad told them I could help change their lives. These are important stories; they explain how I could have so much in common with prospective students whose lives were so different from my own. Our similar experiences speak to a salient tension in the meta-stories we tell about the expansion of for-profit colleges: how could white men in an MBA program have anything in common with the poor black women in a vocational certificate program? How could the for-profit college model work for so many types of people that most corners of society think of as categorically different? Unraveling these intricacies reveals how the rise of for-profit colleges is troubling for all of us. How my own life changed while I was changing theirs—for better or for worse—is where this story begins.

The Beauty College

At the turn of the twenty-first century, college graduates frequently got things called jobs upon graduating. I had gotten a job even before graduating, and I took it. It was a good job, as we commonly define them. It was with a large publicly traded company in the technology sector. Were it the lingo at the time, we would say the company was creating the jobs of the future. While my job may have been at a company that would make the future, my job duties were decidedly retro. I trained the customer service agents you call to start, stop, or fix your cellphone. Cellphone sales were booming. Some people were buying more than one at a time. The telecom giant I worked for could not hire enough people fast enough. Every six weeks, a fresh group of new hires showed up at my corporate classroom, which was housed in a shiny new megacomplex in a new office park in the suburbs of Charlotte. They came in groups of twenty to thirty. They ranged in educational levels, abilities, and experiences. My job was threefold. First, I had to teach the proprietary mapping, programming, and accounting software that the company used. Second, I had to identify the weaklings who couldn't keep up so they could be terminated before their six-week conditional employment period ended. And, finally, I had to teach them how to teach millions of new customers the language of cellphones, the meaning of minutes, bill cycles, upgrades, and phone brands.

I did not know it at the time, but I was living in the telecom bubble, the start of which most experts place at 1997. It was fueled by massive equity investment in telecommunications. You may be thinking Internet, but the real engine behind the bubble was the old-fashioned telephone. A change in the regulation of the providers who bring us our landline telephone service sparked massive amounts of investment, speculation, and valuation of a range of telecommunication services. Whether a company was laying fiber-optic cable or building wireless cellular towers, there seemed to be someone willing to invest. By March 2000, the NASDAQ index of telecommunications stocks had experienced an 84 percent average annual increase for three straight years.[1] That was a phenomenal rate of growth for an industry that writer and technology consultant John Handley described just ten years prior in the book *Telebomb* as one marked by the "sleepy" long-distance service business. Other industry watchers and insiders also used this characterization. Larry Kaufman, one-time public relations director of Southern Pacific, told *Forbes* magazine in 1999 that until billionaire financiers' investment, its telecom business was a "sleepy little operation." [2] Writing for *Bloomberg* financial magazine in 1999, journalist Roger O. Crockett describes the financial machinations behind Bell Atlantic's takeover of telecom properties as one that was attempting "nothing less than the transformation of a sleepy, regional monopoly" that could compete in the telecom gold rush. [3] The ideological framing of sleepy giants awakened by investment and capital accumulation defines the story of how I came to work in the for-profit college sector and a way to understand why for-profit colleges grew so fast.

Advancements in telecom technology provided the backdrop of structural changes that led me to my first interview at a for-profit college. These macro changes in work were fueled by technological change, policy, and financial investment. These are the forces that shape the contexts of our work and personal lives. Credentialism theory suggests that they also explain how and why we pursue credentials. More importantly, these macro contexts shape the type of institutions that provide those credentials, who pays for them, and how we pay for them individually and collectively. Interestingly, descriptions of the telecom bubble by politicians, writers, and researchers before it burst are remarkably similar to descriptions of the Wall Street era of for-profit college expansion. Recall that Handley called pre-1990s telecom "sleepy." Writing of the 1990s-era business of for-profit colleges, *Chronicle of Higher Education* reporter Kim Strosnider said, "Within little more than five years, postsecondary proprietary education has been transformed from a sleepy sector of the economy, best-known for mom-and-pop trade schools, to a $3.5-billion-a-year-business that is increasingly dominated by companies building regional and even national franchises."[4] These industries—telecommunications and higher education—were said to be slumbering giants, waiting for innovation and disruption. The narratives are not only striking for their similarity but also for the way they would eventually intersect. They would lead me from one slumbering industry to another, and the disruption–innovation narrative would help explain who picked up the phone to call someone like me.

By 2000, the telecom bubble was bursting. Increasingly complex financial arrangements had created a silo of short-term gains but poor long-term value. While there were certainly detractors, the prevailing mood of powerful parties around telecom told us we were fools to bet against cellphones, the Internet, and the future. Eventually, however, market conditions soured. By the end of 2000, the telecom NASDAQ index had fallen by 62 percent. In my small corner the changes were swift, noticeable, and terrifying. First, hiring slowed. At the peak, we had hired people in droves during massive job fairs and open houses. You could walk in for an interview and leave with an offer letter. These were not small jobs. Many of the agents would make north of $60,000 annually after shift differential pay and overtime. Some of them had college degrees and even advanced degrees. Many of them did not. They had experience in sales, customer service, or something technically oriented. As the bubble burst, requirements for hiring increased. Applicants had to have more years of experience, degrees went from preferred and unlikely to requirements. Perversely, the knowledge base of those I trained declined as hiring requirements increased. They were likely to have sales experience and maybe an associate's degree. But they were also less likely to have technical knowledge of even basic computer operations. At the peak of the bubble, when hiring was rabid, I could spend the first week of class delving into the differences between CDMA and GSM cellphone technology. As the bubble burst, I could spend a week teaching new hires computer basics. Over the previous two years I had developed a language of "click," "go here," "navigate," and "icon."

Suddenly, one day in class a middle-aged black woman raised her hand. With no small amount of frustration she asked, "What is an icon?!" Her classmates nodded in relief. The questions that followed ranged from "What do you mean by click?" to "Mouse? What does the mouse do?" The best explanation is that while requirements had increased, pay had decreased. This changed the characteristics that the company looked for in new hires. On the frontlines, at least, the conflict between declining pay and job complexity was evident.

As such things go, the quality of my job followed the fortunes of the company. And the company's fortunes were tied up in a global game of capital, financialization, and risk management. I was relieved when I got an unsolicited email from a professional recruiter. The email read: *Dear Ms. McMillan, Your resume matches the desired qualifications of a client that is hiring for a mid-career-level professional in education. Please contact me to discuss details.* This was the golden age before emails such as this were likely to be spam and career overtures were likely to be automated LinkedIn requests. I did not hesitate to respond with my contact information. Within twenty-four hours I had cleared the initial screening with a third-party recruiter. That lent an air of professionalism to a job that sounded like a step up the ladder. The company was national. It operated a "network of professional education providers." It had just completed a "leveraged buyout" of a local group of schools. I would use "state-of-the-art marketing programs" to respond to requests from prospective students. I would be trained in "federal guidelines on grants and loans" and I would have an office with a door.

Before I explain my first experience working in a for-profit college, some context is helpful. Who we are shapes how we experience the world. I am black and a woman. My family is rural in origin, but found itself smack dab in the middle of the Great Migration that moved millions of blacks from the South to the North. My mother was a community organizer. My grandmother had pictures of the good Rev. Dr. Martin Luther King Jr. on the wall. I had a library card by the time I was seven years old. I went to step shows at black colleges with youth groups that had names like Junior Achievement and Upward Bound. I had attended a black college, as had my parents. And, as is common among people with similar demographics, I revered higher education even when I stumbled in attaining it. In fact, I may have revered it all the more because I spent a while being "a few credits shy" of a bachelor's degree. My reverence for education is in line with a wide body of research that finds, when we hold indicators of income and wealth constant, African Americans aspire to levels of educational attainment at rates equal to or greater than their white, Asian, and Hispanic counterparts.[5]

That's who I was when I pulled into the Beauty College's parking lot in 2002. I was living the anxiety of the massive structural change in how we work. I had never heard of a for-profit college, though I had heard of beauty colleges. Everyone from where I am from has heard of beauty colleges. When you could not afford to visit a regular salon, staffed by licensed beauticians, you visited the local beauty college to be styled by students. The rates were cheap. The service was horrendous. You could leave with half the hair you came in with or leave looking like a dream; it was a risk you took for a 60 percent discount. While I had no aspirations to be a cosmetologist, being an admissions counselor at a school was something altogether different. The recruiter said the company executives liked my work experience. I thought they were referring to my years spent training agents throughout the country for employment with the Fortune 500 telecom company. Charlie set me straight.

Charlie was the executive vice president of admissions and marketing for the Beauty College. He was tall on the top and short on the bottom. Charlie walked fast and had a really sharp crease in his dress pants. I thought he was Italian. He was Jewish. I was Southern, and the differences weren't particularly salient to me.

The fact that Charlie was a New Yorker mattered a lot to how I understood him. In my experience, he was a classic New Yorker of the second- or third-generation variety. He had television teeth, and he showed them a lot. His inky black curls looked like they could be snapped off like fresh string beans before you put them in a hot pot. I decided that presentation and deference and being efficient would matter to Charlie, the New Yorker. He looked me up and down in the waiting room, told me I was "sharp," and ushered me into an office with a door. For the next thirty minutes Charlie described the Beauty College by explaining to me how good he was at running at it.

Charlie said that he had invented something called Accu-track. He slid a printout across the desk to me. Accu-track *accurately tracked* all incoming calls to the Beauty College. The printout looked like a screenshot of an Excel table. It had five or six columns, the first of which was a ten-digit phone number. It also gave you the start time of the call, how long the call lasted, and an empty space to assign a resolution to the call. Charlie was very impressed with his system. It had revolutionized the pen-and-paper mayhem of the Beauty College's parent company. That parent company was family-owned and had been regionally focused for decades. The family had recently decided to branch out and offer more students a chance at a new life. Charlie had been hired to modernize operations and to discipline the admissions process. Accu-track was the key to both. Being the creator of Accu-track gave Charlie a lot of company clout. I know that because he told me.

Charlie also told me how the admissions process worked by telling me for whom it worked. The Beauty College had pinpointed its likely student. "They're sitting at home in the middle of the day," Charlie said. They are watching judge shows at 2 p.m. or repeats at 11 p.m. They have a screaming baby or maybe a bad husband. They are tired and overwhelmed. They are shy. They are scared of authority. They need help. You could tell who needed it most by using the time stamps on the Accu-track. "See these—fifteen . . .

twenty seconds?" Charlie said, stabbing at the printout. "There's no voicemail message at those times, and the call is too short to leave a message. Those are the ones who need us most." The people who would call and hang up needed the Beauty College most, and Accu-track could quantify that with a time stamp. Charlie paused and looked at me expectantly. I parroted back, "They hang up, too afraid to even leave a message?" Charlie crowed. I got it. I understood.

My job would be to get those students over their fear, he said. The first thing you did was you called that phone number until someone answered. Because Accu-track only gave numbers—no names—you spoke to whomever answered the phone. You asked if they had called about school. If they hadn't, you asked if they had thought about school. You got a name, any name that you could use on follow-up phone calls. You had one goal: get the person on the other end to set up a time to do a campus interview. A number was "live" on Accu-track until it had become a campus interview.

Charlie modeled the interview process for me. Ask closed-ended questions. Create a "pattern of yes." Understand what is holding them back. Give them a solution. Give them only *one* solution. Get them to sign an enrollment agreement and set up another appointment to finish the process. You *wanted* multiple appointments. It was key to the process. Get them to come back for a second financial aid appointment. If they don't keep the appointment, call them to get them back in. My job, Charlie said, was to train students how to show up at a place every day precisely when they were expected to show up. These types of students, he said, did not always understand that concept. After a mock interview, Charlie gave me a tour of the facility as he would give it to a prospective student. The tour was focused on how clean the place was and how all the hair tools were included in the tuition.

Tuition. It wasn't until after the tour that Charlie got down to those kinds of details with me. The nine-month program cost just north of $15,000. The Beauty School did not guarantee that students would pass the state-licensing exam that was legally required in order to work as a cosmetologist. However, students could come back to the school for free and practice until they passed. The tuition was a little more than twice that of area cosmetology schools, like the privately owned for-profit Dudley's Beauty College, where I had been a client many times growing up.[6] Before I could ask, Charlie explained the tuition as an ultimate cost-saver for students, even if the absolute cost was far higher than that of competitors. It was all about "upfronts," or the immediate out-of-pocket expenses, as opposed to amortized costs over time.

Our students could not afford the $1,200 cash deposit that most competitors demanded, or the $500 to $700 obligatory monthly payments to stay enrolled for the duration of the certificate program. Also, those other programs did not provide cosmetology equipment. New employers don't either. A sign of professionalism in the cosmetology profession is for one to show up with one's own tools. A complete set of hair straighteners, irons, and accoutrements can cost $350 alone. Unlike students who would, by choice or work location, primarily do Caucasian hair, those who expected to have a more diverse client base needed such tools. Those students were more likely to be black and Hispanic; they were the least likely to have the personal or family means to invest in upfronts but needed the tools the most.[7] That was how Charlie had siphoned off a largely African American student base for a school that specialized in styling Caucasian hair in a city with at least three well-known, historically black beauty colleges like Dudley's Beauty College: he offered students a chance to finance their education and get their tools with minimal upfront costs. It was the first tricky way that cumulative disadvantage would factor into my experience of for-profit colleges, but it would not be the last.

I left that day with a promise that I would get a call. I got the call that night. I was an admissions counselor at a beauty school.

That's how I said it, because that is how I experienced it. Charlie never said the words "for-profit college" or "proprietary college" to me. It wasn't anywhere in the nineteen-page enrollment agreement I scanned during the mock student interview. It wasn't on the shiny two-pocket folder into which I would slide sheets with career statistics and job-placement data for students to take home. I would work at the Beauty College for almost two years, and those words would never be said—not at regional admissions meetings, national trainings, or weekly "numbers" calls. We were counselors. We helped people. And we were a school. To know differently would be to be different—different people, with different experiences and different knowledge about higher education and prestige. Even with "almost enough college credits" from a real college and years of college prep programs and indoctrination into the education gospel, I had no framework by which to understand school as anything other than a social good for which one could never pay too much. That belief wouldn't be challenged until I experienced the Technical College.

The Technical College

If the Beauty College helped people, the Technical College sold people. I didn't end up at the Technical College immediately after leaving the Beauty College. There was a great step in the middle where I worked in advertising, writing copy and working with clients. By the time I landed at the Technical College, I had finished up those remaining college credit hours and a marriage. It was only a matter of time before I thought about once again "moving up." I was still just thinking about it when, yet again, a recruiter contacted me about a job in admissions. I did not want to go back to a career-oriented school. The pay was fine for the nature of the job, but I had learned that it was hard to compensate for the emotional labor of enrolling students who needed so much more than we could give them. I held babies during appointments. I drove students across state lines to cajole reticent parents into signing financial aid paperwork. I stood in line with students at bureaucratic offices to help them get a copy of their birth certificate or a Social Security card. I drove them home when a boyfriend did not show up at the end of the night with the car that almost always belonged to my student, his girlfriend. I smoothed over miscommunications between students and their welfare caseworkers, making up the paperwork they needed to stay benefits-eligible (with proof of "college" enrollment in an "occupationally oriented program"). That very essential care work was inspired by the students with whom I worked, not by the type of school that employed me. I still did not know what a for-profit college was.

However, I did know what $10,000 more in pay was, I knew what job security meant, and I had a clue about tuition reimbursement. The recruiter who emailed me about the job at the Technical College promised me all of those things. Unlike the Beauty College, the Technical College conferred *real* degrees in a language I understood: bachelor's and master's degrees in information technology and business administration. I interviewed with the director of enrollment. James was as unlike Charlie as the Beauty College was unlike the Technical College. Where Charlie had a practiced street-wise shtick and was proud of his hands-on knowledge of career schools, James had a professional naïveté cultivated through his social distance from the nuts and bolts of what the Technical College did. Charles preferred Charlie and, to stay in the thick of things, regaled me with stories of closing students. James preferred James, and his background was in accounting and finance. James had little interest in the day-to-day operation of enrollment at the Technical College. James wanted the daily, weekly, and monthly enrollment numbers and absolutely zero fires to put out. He liked my client management experience, which is what you call sales when you had to get a degree to do the job. And he salivated over my interview outfit, a black dress and pumps. He

3) you can fill in the bubbles without wearing a hole in the paper. I filled out the assessment. One-third of the questions were about the job duties—the campus tour, the interview, the enrollment agreement—and two-thirds were about company, state and federal policies, and penalties governing how we enrolled students. I could not, under any circumstances, call myself an admissions officer. We enrolled; we did not admit. We could not disclose tuition information over the phone or before giving a prospective student a tour of the facilities. We could sit in the room with a student as they completed their federal financial aid forms, but I could not press any buttons (if completed online) or put pen to paper to help the student. I could tell students about "grants and aid available," but I could not discuss loan terms or servicing options.

I finished the assessment in an hour and a half. I flipped through the training manual until Lisa hustled by, taking short, quick steps and shouting, "Make those calls!" She was surprised that I had finished so soon and was more than a little pissed off. But she graded the assessment, proclaimed that I had passed, and then began the real training. Lisa had faith in three things: markets, her jeep, and closing a sale. She did not care about "sob stories" or education as a social good. She was quite clear on that. Lisa pulled out some marketing materials and began demonstrating how the sales process at the Technical College worked.

First, each enrollment officer received a list of leads every day that they were to "work." Working the leads meant calling until someone answered and talking until someone agreed to come in for a campus tour. The best leads went to the best closers, like Robert. Robert was a former college football player. He dressed sharply, and Lisa was slightly bedazzled by the effect. She said Robert knew how to talk to "these students" and he had closed (read: enrolled) his first student his second day on the job. I would sit beside Robert, even though Lisa doubted I had the stuff to compete with him. It was an empty spot with a phone. I wouldn't get high-quality leads like Robert's unless and until I had proved that I could close. High-quality leads had come from somewhere that could affix a name to a phone number. Another enrollment adviser had worked them first. Thus, these leads would often have some notes affixed. Those notes were what made a lead high quality. They included details that helped a new enrollment adviser quickly establish rapport: a child's name, where the prospect worked, what team they rooted for. Closers got those leads.

Rubes and slowpokes got lower-quality leads. Some had names (I still had no idea where those names came from, but more on that later) and some looked more like Charlie's Accu-track leads; i.e., just phone numbers, most without any time stamps of previous calls. These leads were supposedly fresher than trash leads, but not as fresh as high-quality leads. Freshness denoted how long the lead had sat unworked or how long it had floated around the enrollment ecosystem without getting a human on the other end of the line. At the bottom were the trash leads. Trash leads came to you on cards or scraps of paper. Like dust, trash leads seemed to always be there, moving from one surface to another and finding their way back to the desk you had just cleaned. These were numbers, culled from god-knows-where by god-knows-who.[9] They were mobile numbers that were disconnected, business lines, and people who had told you to stop calling them. The chances of getting a close from a trash lead seemed to be in line with lottery odds.

Lisa picked out a high-quality lead, pulled a chair up to the table only to prop a foot on it instead of her behind, and commenced showing me how it was done. When the prospect answered the phone, Lisa put on a warm, sunny voice. But she kept her clipped cadence. Lisa sounded young, something I would learn later that she hated almost as much as she loved her jeep. She compensated for her youthful voice by saying her title—director—repeatedly. She told the prospect that the director rarely calls, but that she was special. Lisa understood that she had been thinking about criminal justice and, well, fall was just weeks away. Wouldn't the prospect's friends be going away to college soon, and wouldn't she want to keep up with them? The prospect thought about that for a moment, but Lisa had already barreled ahead. "Look, to get you started in fall like your friends you need to see me this week. We can *maybe* get you into a class in August if you're serious about your paperwork and you keep your appointments." I knew from my training manual that classes started on a rolling basis, with a new start date every three weeks. August wasn't full, and neither were July or June. But Lisa had found a "hook": the connection between fall and college going. It was irrelevant that the semester system did not work that way at the Technical College. The semester system is how college works in the public imagination, and imagination is what Lisa was working, not details.

The prospect had a job. The details of that job escape my notes and memory. I do know that Lisa seized on that bit of information. Did she like her job? Didn't her job suck? Her job was a dead end; was she serious about getting her life together or not? Her friends wouldn't be working dead-end jobs after going to college. Did she want her friends to leave her behind? "Are you serious about this or not? Because I'm the director here, and I have other things to do." In an instant, Lisa had gone from a chummy, albeit overbearing, friend to an authority figure from hell. The switch was part of her toolkit. All of the successful closers at the Technical College had a version of this switch. It was the moment when they disoriented students with a role shift or reversal. Maria, another enrollment adviser, was middle-aged and motherly. She could go from friendly ally to disappointed matriarch in a flash. Michael was a military veteran with the quiet confidence that seems to go with that. He could go from caring listener to silent judge when a prospect waffled. Robert, the super closer, code-switched with remarkable ease. Code-switching is the practice of alternating between two or more languages, or varieties of language, in conversation. It is most commonly used to describe how minorities switch from the coded language, mannerisms, and references of their cultural group to that of the dominant cultural group.[10] Black, male, and equipped with an MBA from a traditional flagship state college, Robert could speak the language Lisa could hear. But he could also switch to the language of his poor black Southern home and urban-casual drug-dealing youth in order to build rapport with prospects to whom that would feel familiar.

By the end of the call, Lisa had convinced the prospect to commit to a campus tour that week. Several of the enrollment advisers had gathered around to observe the demonstration. The audience seemed to amp up the energy of the call. Lisa tossed the information sheet with the lead's name, contact information, and appointment time to an enrollment adviser. The appointment would be the adviser's, not Lisa's. It was a gift of sorts, but it also made it clear that Lisa was in charge. She did not need the close. She was the director. Her job wasn't to close prospects; rather, in a sense, her aim was to close us, the enrollment advisers. Lisa had sold the prospect on a campus tour, but she did it in order to sell us on a way of doing the job that suited the company's focus on enrollment numbers. I could not shake the sense that we were the real prospects being sold.

A River of Dreams:
The For-Profit College Landscape

In neither job did I ever hear the term "for-profit college" uttered even once. In that way, I was like the majority of Americans for whom the term holds little salience.[11] Public Agenda (with the Kresge Foundation) conducted a survey of employers and for-profit college students in 2012.[12] They found that about half of the employers surveyed see few differences between for-profit and not-for-profit colleges. That means many people cannot or do not express that "for-profit college" is a meaningful distinction.

Granted, the other half typically views public institutions as superior on a number of counts. For example, 41 percent say public universities do a better job of preparing students to work at their organizations. But even more striking was that among current for-profit students, 65 percent do not know that they attend a for-profit college, and 63 percent of alumni cannot identify their former institution as a for-profit.

Because I had not heard of the term *for-profit college*, I certainly never used it with prospective students. Like me, most of the prospects I worked with at the Beauty College and the Technical College had little reason to question what makes a school a school. At the Beauty College, prospective students were choosing a program based on their interest in hair and their desire for a decent wage. More than one student, almost all of whom were women, told me that she wanted a "good job" where she could look nice at work and provide for her family. Demographically, the students at the Beauty College were characteristic of those who enroll in short-term certificate programs at for-profit "career" colleges that have clear-cut occupational outcomes: beauty schools, trucking schools, mechanic schools, and medical billing schools. Historically and presently, for-profit colleges have dominated in conferring these short-term certificates.[13] Harvard researchers David J. Deming, Claudia Goldin, and Lawrence F. Katz say, "Completions in the for-profit sector are still dominated by certificate programs and 55 percent of the certificates granted by the for-profits are awarded by the 1,700 or so independent career colleges and institutes." Those enrolled in such programs at for-profit colleges are more likely to be black, Hispanic, and female than are students enrolled in degree-granting for-profit colleges.[14]

The data are stark anyway you cut it, but it is important to point out that the overall for-profit college sector is browner, poorer, older, and more likely to be female than are traditional colleges.

Deming et al. describe the for-profit college student population thusly:

> The for-profit sector disproportionately serves older students, women, African Americans, Hispanics, and those with low incomes. African Americans account for 13 percent of all students in higher education, but they are 22 percent of those in the for-profit sector. Hispanics are 15 percent of those in the for-profit sector, yet 11.5 percent of all students. Women are 65 percent of those in the for-profit sector. For-profit students are older, about 65 percent are 25 years and older, whereas just 31 percent of those at four-year public colleges are and 40 percent of those at two-year colleges are.[15]

Even in a sector that disproportionately enrolls disadvantaged students, the most disadvantaged are concentrated in certificate programs. Those were the students at the Beauty College. Their disadvantages showed up in myriad ways: why they called, why they enrolled, why they finished or dropped out, and what the term "for-profit college" would have meant to them, if that phrase were ever to appear in the Beauty College's lexicon.

On the other end of the spectrum, the Technical College was in many ways the type of for-profit college that shaped the public's image of such schools. The Technical College spent more time telling me about regulations because it had been sued or censured many times for violating them. The cycle of regulation, scandal, and deregulation that had trickled down to a new hire like me is characteristic of this Wall Street era of for-profit colleges. The era began with massive private investment in existing for-profit colleges, most of which were small or regional chains that specialized in vocational education (like the regional, family-owned Beauty College that bought out the smaller chain where I would eventually work). This massive financial investment required revenues that would justify that investment. To meet that requirement, shareholder organizations emerged to manage growth strategies. These growth strategies included acquiring other colleges, expanding program offerings, and enrolling more students while keeping operating costs low.[16] Most shareholder for-profit colleges do this by centralizing expenditures.

For example, Strayer University notes in its shareholder disclosures that adding new programs is made less expensive by having a curriculum development team at the national office develop all the course materials. Those materials can be shipped to new faculty for new programs across the country, saving the expense of training faculty on new tools or platforms used to design academic curricula and faculty labor designing those curricula. For-profit colleges also minimize real estate costs through various means, including leasing space in office parks rather than owning and developing their own campuses.[17] Cost savings were reserved for investors, never for students, as shareholder for-profit colleges kept tuition rates sufficiently high to extract maximum federal student aid dollars.[18]

The Beauty College was reminiscent of the for-profit college sector's earlier, quainter days. It was family run. It had deep ties to local groups and a reputation among community members. Sure, there had been some capital leveraging, with one family-run business taking over another to expand. But there were no shareholders and therefore no shareholder demands. This shaped the way the Beauty College recruited and retained students. Ultimately, it shaped how much the Beauty College commodified students' inequalities. In contrast, the Technical College was the apotheosis of today's for-profit college sector—what some people propose will be the future for all of higher education. It was financialized, meaning its operations were embedded in the norms and practices of the financial sector. It was owned by a shareholder corporation. That means it had a corporate structure designed to protect shareholder interests. School administrators like James were not educators. They were finance guys. Many had attended some of the nation's best colleges. Or, at least, they had overwhelmingly attended traditional not-for-profit colleges. They had majors in things like business, marketing, finance, and law.

In 2012, I did a study of the educational biographies of for-profit college executives compared with those of not-for-profit college leaders. First, I looked at the leaders of the "best" colleges as ranked by *U.S. News and World Report* (USNWR) in 2011. These were all not-for-profit colleges. I took the top three from that list. However, higher education is more diverse and much larger than the handful of prestigious brand-name schools that most of us know about. For a better comparison, I also looked at USNWR's lists for best national schools, best liberal arts schools, best schools for B students, and schools with the highest number of commuter students. Of the twelve traditional colleges, all but one was led by a former college faculty member who possessed a PhD from a traditional college. Their disciplines varied from physics to literature, but across the board, to lead even a commuter college one has to have a traditional terminal degree from a not-for-profit college. In contrast, out of the leaders of eight publicly traded shareholder for-profit colleges, only three had presidents with a PhD at the time: the University of Phoenix, Strayer University, and Argosy University. Two of the for-profit presidents did not have a degree higher than a bachelor's degree, and one had an MBA. Only one had a degree from a for-profit college: Craig D. Swenson of Argosy University, who had earned a PhD. from for-profit Walden University.

In another study, one I completed as a part of my PhD dissertation, I examined the backgrounds of the officers listed on the documents that for-profit colleges file with the Securities and Exchange Commission (SEC) to become shareholder companies. I looked at all the financial documents filed during the Wall Street era for every such shareholder for-profit college. These documents included biographies of the executive boards. The expectation is that these boards will guide and reflect shareholder interests, which can be described simply as generating a profit while minimizing external disruptions to profit (bumps in the road, such as investigations or lawsuits).

According to these biographies, 87 percent of the officers were from the fields of finance or business. They had titles like equity manager and chief operating officer and worked in a range of occupations loosely related to moving capital around to buy and sell things. The Technical College where I worked was part of this tradition. Its leader was not an academic with a PhD. He was a business guy. The business guy had hired a finance guy to manage enrollment numbers at the local campus. And the business guy had hired Lisa, who loved markets and was enrolled in an online MBA at for-profit Strayer University, to handle the details of enrollment. From the top to the front lines, business and finance shaped how we did our jobs at the Technical College. The Technical College commodified a different yet interlocking set of inequalities than those at the Beauty College. Beauty College prospects were persistently poor or dancing along that line of poverty and working poor. Technical College prospects had some college credits, some working-class job experiences, and even some aspects of middle-class consumption. Many were already working, while Beauty College prospects rarely were. More of the prospects at the Technical College were male and white. Almost all of the students at the Beauty College were female and came from a range of racial and ethnic backgrounds, with African American women forming a slight majority. Beauty College prospects rarely showed up with parents. Technical College prospects did so more often. At the Beauty College, we welcomed parents when they did show up. At the Beauty College, parental participation signaled that the student was invested in completing enrollment and was likely to graduate. At the Technical College, parents were often disdained. They were roadblocks to closing; hence, prospects with parents tagging along got shorter tours and softer sells.

Why these differences matter and how they relate to inequality

are the questions I eventually took away from my time at the two
for-profit colleges, each college resting at one of the two poles that
pull, shape, and constrain the sector that sells education for profit.
These two schools are exemplars of the social processes that condition students differently for different kinds of education. More
important, these processes emerge from job conditions and macro
shifts in risks from states and corporations to people.

There are two widely known academic works about how and
why some students end up at elite colleges and others do not.
The first is *The Shape of the River: Long-Term Consequences of
Considering Race in University Admissions* by William G. Bowen
(a former president of Princeton University and of the Andrew
W. Mellon Foundation) and Derek Bok (a former president of
Harvard University). In it, they try to evaluate the effectiveness
of affirmative action. They argue that there is a river that carries
some people along the path of upward mobility or, at least, pre-
vents downward mobility. Affirmative action, they argue, helps
introduce African Americans—long deprived of access to the pre-
conditions of college admissions and to college—to that river at a
"tolerable" social cost. Douglas Massey, Camille Charles, Garvey
Lundy, and Mary Fischer followed up some years later with *The
Source of the River: The Social Origins of Freshman at America's
Selective Colleges and Universities*. They took the river metaphor
and tried to measure which parts of the river carry minority students to the Ivy League and which don't. The book was also about
race-based affirmative action.[19] While the story of for-profit colleges in the new economy isn't exactly about affirmative action,
the way these important scholarly books characterize how to understand the ways institutions and macro systems and different
groups of students interact with each other to create credentialing
phenomena is very helpful for our purposes.

One reason these books spawned numerous studies and debates about college access, equity, and social mobility is because
the river metaphor is very useful for understanding how inequal-

ity works. When you are born to an upper social class in the United States, you have to work hard *not* to go to college. When you are born poor, you have to work quite hard for college to be a real option. Who we are is part of a complex network of family ties, social connections, schools, ideologies, and expectations that shape our individual motivations. Like swimming upstream, it is always easier to go with the flow, whether or not that's the best course for every fish in the sea. There is a tendency across research, social policy, and public discourse on for-profit colleges to treat the sector as a single entity. (Research by sociologist Charlie Eaton and a 2012 report by the Institute for Higher Education Policy are notable exceptions.) That would mean one river carries middle-class, white-collar workers to the MBA program at Capella and the poor black mother of three who is close to maxing out her welfare eligibility to the cosmetology certificate at Empire Beauty School. The Beauty School students and the Technical College students typically don't share a social class, an income bracket, or the same kind of social and cultural capital. All of our traditional means of thinking about those students as a single group break down.

How can the same river be carrying these varied students to Lower Ed? Here is where a different theory than those usually used in academic and policy research is helpful. Sociologists have developed the idea of credentialing theory or credentialism to understand the complex interplay between macro social and economic changes, how groups experience those changes, and how systems produce new credentials en masse to navigate those changes. Perhaps more than theories that focus on who students are or cost-benefit analyses of individual students' choices, credentialing theory illuminates the arguably counterintuitive decisions people make. What if students end up in Lower Ed not because of who they are, but because of how the new economy is changing how we work? What if white-collar men and blue-collar women are similarly vulnerable to stagnating wages, declining job quality, and flattened career ladders, and differ only in the resources that they have to adapt to and weather these challenges?

That would mean that there is in fact one river with two streams made of social origins—family, education, income, wealth, and social know-how—that determine if you go to the Technical College or the Beauty College. But as one river, these streams flow through a single valley—a time trap where the risk shift of educational costs outstrip social insurance programs like affordable childcare, the viability of investment vehicles like education savings accounts, and employer security like promotions and wage increases. For millions of people, the time trap makes a for-profit college your only practical choice for labor market entry, stability, or mobility.

This is how I came to see the landscape and expansion of for-profit higher education through the lens of increasing inequality. The lesson is multifold. First, it is difficult to ascertain how labor markets and education credentials and what we call extra-institutional policies like welfare and childcare are related. There are so many variables that it is hard to pinpoint the relationships between those variables in the kinds of data sets we have long used to measure economic activity and educational pathways. That's why really ambitious researchers like Sara Goldrick-Rab take on developing complex studies that gather experiences as well as quantitative measures for those experiences.[20] Goldrick-Rab's book *Paying the Price* draws on years of data from how low-income students pay for college. The premise is that understanding how the federal financial aid system works for the most vulnerable students tells us how the system should be reformed. Goldrick-Rab follows a group of students who use financial aid to pay for college—as over half of all students now do—just after the Great Recession. As in this book, the economic context matters to how vulnerable students *experience* the system of financial aid.

The lesson for policy is that we need more such research and data. Also, the complexities of interrelated processes are, by nature, experiential. When there is a measurable, sustained change in a system like higher education we must re-evaluate how we come to understand the phenomenon. That means departing from the methods that we developed to study previous systems and processes to make sure they still measure what we think they measure.

To do that, we must start with the experience of the phenomenon. How does "choosing" a for-profit college feel for the students who choose them? And, in what ways are those choices shaped by shifting institutional characteristics and our relationship to them? In effect, the lesson of the for-profit college phenomenon is that there is *always value in revisiting the source of the river.* In the coming chapters, I explore the experience of choosing a for-profit college from the perspectives of students who are likely to lose as a result and from those who are by all measures "winning" the complex game of low-prestige, high-risk, high-cost higher educational choices. These students' experiences show how shifting risk from states and companies to workers and students undermines the premise of the education gospel. As it turns out, there is such a thing as "bad" education. It is an educational option that, by design, cannot increase students' odds of beating the circumstances of their birth. I then recreate the experience of enrolling in a for-profit college like those that dominated the sector at the turn of the 2000s. This experience shows how choice is a complicated notion, full of assumptions based on class, race, and gender. Finally, I argue that when the outcomes of labor market changes are knowable, the public has its own choice to make. In the case of the new economy, the labor market ethos is clear: more, better, faster workers produced cheaply at little to no expense for companies and speculators. As the public, we once chose to let shareholder for-profit colleges promise to do just that. The evidence is in on that promise. For-profit colleges do not have employment or wage returns that justify their cost to either students or our public system of financial aid. That leaves us with the question of just how we should proceed with reclaiming security for U.S. workers in the new economy.

Next, I will examine the character and behavior of the Lower Ed river. Chapter 3 is full of boats, rafts, and life preservers. It details how students are delivered to the Beauty College and the Technical College—how they are recruited and enrolled, how they experience college, and what happens to them when they leave.

3

JESUS IS MY BACKUP PLAN

All of higher education involves risk. But we accept that risk if we think that the best-case scenario is one worth the worst-case scenario. We accept that a small, selective group of young adults will go to Harvard every year. Admission to a college like Harvard is associated with all kinds of rewards: great social esteem, likelihood of well-paying work, the financial freedom to pursue meaningful work, and the right to say one went to that school in Boston. Few of us will make it to Harvard. Few of us will have children who make it to Harvard. But knowing that some young person not born to privilege will, on occasion, make it to Harvard is part of why we put our faith in the vast, stratified system of higher education institutions that span community colleges to the Ivy League. If the for-profit college industry offers the same kind of risk scenario, then its best-case scenario would be one that justifies for us the worst-case scenario: indebted students with poor job prospects and little esteem or meaningful work for the risk that they took on higher education. Mike is the best-case scenario.

The Hustle

Lenox Mall in Atlanta, Georgia, is the most upscale mall in a city with at least a dozen from which to choose. Behind each of the city's shopping destinations is a history of gentrifying

neighborhoods, shifting demographics, and urban sprawl and re-
newal plans. Lenox is the mall your out-of-town guests want to
visit. It is anchored by Neiman Marcus and has storefronts for
brands rarely seen outside of New York and Los Angeles. Lenox
Mall is the crystallization of the "city too busy to hate," a new urban South core where being rich and black in America is a ten-year
plan.[1] It is hard to get to Lenox Mall no matter how close you are
to it. Five miles may as well be thirty with Atlanta traffic and the
confusing web of exit ramps and sudden lane changes. For that
reason, I visited Lenox Mall only a dozen times in the half decade
or so that I lived in Atlanta. On one such occasion I was, as usual,
poorly dressed for the fancy mall. I was knee-deep in planning my
dissertation and preparing to move for a fellowship. I wanted to be
anywhere but Lenox Mall until I overheard Mike talking to Sean
at the parking deck entrance.

I had stopped to take a picture of the entrance so that I wouldn't
lose my car (again) when I heard one of the two young black men
tell the other, "No, see, your loan refund comes in like one week,
maybe two." My ears were primed for that kind of talk. Not only
was it squarely in my wheelhouse on student loan debt research,
but it was happening between two black men out in public. As a
sociologist, that is akin to hitting two of three pineapples on the
slots in Vegas. I lingered to do some eavesdropping, or what pro-
fessionally we call ethnographic research. The shorter of the two
men was Atlanta sharp, wearing a soft pink dress shirt with cuff
links, jeans, and shoes whose name I couldn't recall but that were
supple enough to suggest the fault was mine. He went on to tell
his taller and equally natty friend about how easy it was to enroll
in the MBA program at Strayer University, a large for-profit college brand. I started tying my shoes to stretch the moment. The
taller friend, Sean, worried about the coursework. "Man, I know
a girl who can give you all the homework and assignments for
the classes," his friend reassured him. He went on to explain that
the interest rates were low and the penalty for borrowing money

to "flip" into a business venture was offset by how easy it was to access.

When I tell this story to academic audiences, they are frequently aghast. The idea of using student loan money for anything other than school seems wrong to many people. Some have gone so far as to call it theft, even when the money is spent on things that help one stay in school, like childcare or getting a car fixed.[2] But for many others the very idea of a student loan refund or stipend check is foreign. Let's take a brief moment to discuss how and why that is.

I could say the words "student loan refund check" to African Americans with any postsecondary education experience and likely be understood. I tested this out. I was so certain about the salience of the term that in writing this book it never occurred to me to explain it. There is an entire cultural language about the refund check. Black people have jokes about how they spent it and true stories of how it saved them from homelessness, hunger, or illness. Alas, when I said student loan refund check to someone from a different background, it did not resonate at all. I asked around. Many people did not know the term and could not ascertain its meaning from the context. Some of these people had attended college in the 1960s and 1970s. That makes sense, as the calculation on which the term is based did not exist until 1972 changes to the Higher Education Act. Others had attended college later but had parents who paid for college. Or they had full scholarships or some other direct means of paying tuition and living while in college. Others did not recognize the term but after reflection realized that they had gotten some money back from their college. They didn't know why or how it worked. For thousands of students who rely most on federal student grants and loans to pay for college, the refund check is critical.

Students can, of course, borrow more than the cost of their tuition from federal student aid. Colleges and universities even publish both their tuition amount and what is called the "estimated

cost of attendance" or COA. The COA includes estimates for
things like books, housing, and food.[3] The estimates vary from
institution to institution and are different for undergraduate
versus graduate or professional school. There is evidence that for-
profit colleges estimate far higher costs of attendance than not-
for-profit colleges in the same geographic region. Researchers with
the Wisconsin Hope Lab found that not-for-profit community
colleges and public universities, on average, *underestimate* costs
while for-profit colleges are "providing living cost allowances that
exceed living cost estimates by $3,000."[4] Students may then bor-
row up to the total cost of attendance at school after all other aid
has been applied. To get a refund a student is likely poor enough to
get grant money that pays part of the tuition or to have a scholar-
ship or some other form of aid. That money is applied first to one's
bill, as it were. After that, a student can borrow the maximum allowed by Federal Student Aid limits and have an overpayment on
their account. This results in a scenario where one has a refund.
These refunds, or overages, are meant to be used for costs associated with school attendance. Goldrick-Rab finds that the poorest
students not only rely on this refund system for cash transfers but
they use it to support their parents and extended social networks.
I understood Mike and Sean instantly in Lenox Mall that day because the language of financial aid refund checks was culturally
salient for me. I have lived on a refund check.

Many in higher education or those who have not borrowed to
attend college consider borrowing more than the price of tuition
a moral issue. But, as I was once told and am fond of telling my
students, assigning blame can get in the way of understanding
complex social phenomena. Few phenomena are as complex as the
question of why students, especially those with the acumen to attend a traditional college, would go to a for-profit college. Mike
was just such a case and part of his decision-making was based
on how seamlessly he could get a student loan refund at Strayer. I
eventually introduced myself to the two young men in the Lenox

Mall parking lot. I handed them a card and apologized for eaves-dropping. I explained my research interests and begged them to let me buy them a cup of coffee and talk. Sean had places to be, but the shorter one, Mike, had time and the inclination to "network." A few hours later, Mike and I were talking about what he called the hustle.

Mike was thirty-two years old at the time. He had a bache-lor's degree from Morehouse College, a historically black college (or HBCU) that is storied among students from that tradition. Dr. Martin Luther King Jr. attended Morehouse, as did hundreds of black men who would go on to be central figures in every-thing from politics to business. A "Morehouse Man" is one who is not just educated but also savvy about class mobility. While the Morehouse Man mystique can be critiqued for perpetuating a bourgeoisie, heteronormative idea of black masculinity, that it is even debated speaks to how powerful the idea is among many black Americans. Mike was the quintessential Morehouse Man. He was well dressed and articulate. He was at Lenox Mall on a Tuesday afternoon meeting a friend to talk business and buy new shirts. He accepted my eavesdropping graciously and called me ma'am. He also intuited an opportunity to connect with a po-tentially useful contact, a black woman working on her PhD at a prestigious local university. None of that was lost on me when we talked. Before we got to the conversation about Strayer University, Mike ran through whom I might know, where I was from, and how PhD programs work. Fair is fair, so I answered his questions before posing a few of my own.

First, I wanted to know, why Strayer? Atlanta has one of the highest densities of higher education options of any U.S. met-ropolitan area.[5] Atlanta also holds an esteemed position in the collective memory and current imagination of black Americans. It has long been a city with significant local black political lead-ership. It was a key staging area for the black civil rights move-ment. It has 8 of the country's 107 historically black colleges and

universities within 100 miles of the city's downtown core.[6] If there
is anywhere in the nation where one might safely assume that a
young black man has the cultural capital—or the know-how—
to navigate the complex higher education landscape of prestige
and debt, it would be Atlanta, Georgia. Yet that assumption pre-
sumes to know Mike, and it would be wrong. Mike said, "Why
not Strayer?" when I asked him if the school felt like it was in a
different class than Morehouse or even neighboring public college Georgia State University. "You mean because it's online?" he
asked. I hemmed and hawed in my response, as I often did at this
moment in interviewing people.

An online college can be a for-profit college, but not all for-
profit colleges are online, and not all online colleges are for-
profit colleges. But, as it is for many Americans, the distinction
was meaningless to Mike.[7] If I explained the difference, I risked
priming different responses from the people I talked to than they
would arrive at naturally. It became a real conundrum throughout
my research interviews and fieldwork. Finally, I settled on asking how Strayer was different from Morehouse. "Oh [*laughter*],
Morehouse is a real college. I mean . . . it's *Morehouse*," Mike replied. Different how, exactly? "Well, you know," he continued, "it's
an HBCU. We're one of the best colleges in the country. I always
knew I was going to Morehouse. I mean . . ." Mike had difficulty
settling on the words to describe how Morehouse was different
than Strayer. He was not alone. Almost every student I talked to
had a hard time explaining how their for-profit college was different from traditional colleges. There were frequent allusions to
traditional colleges being "real," even when the students would go
on to argue that their for-profit college was far superior. Others,
like Mike, grasped that a for-profit college (or online school, as all
but 3 of the 109 students I interviewed called them interchange-
ably, even when they attended on-campus) was somehow distinct.
And, like Mike, many of them relied on our both being black and
college educated to intuit the difference.

Mike meant that Morehouse College is not just a place to earn a degree or to develop a skill that might be valuable in the job market. It is not, to revisit Grubb and Lazerson's education gospel, merely a vocational project. Morehouse College is a tradition. Even if you are the first in your family to go to college (Mike was not) or the first in your family to attend Morehouse (Mike was), the symbolism of institutional tradition was communicated to you in a thousand ways, both large and small. Morehouse College has a recognizable brand name and paraphernalia, often distributed during prospective student visits. Visiting Morehouse is an experience. Prospects don't just sit in on classes or tour the dorms. Enthusiastic college representatives teach prospects the college chants. From the first engagement with the college, prospects are told what it means to be a Morehouse Man. It is a narrative about being moral and ambitious; envied and upwardly mobile; fortunate and civically responsible. It is like the experience at hundreds of traditional colleges across the United States, but it is specific to a black tradition. Faith and church are important cornerstones of black institutions, and Morehouse is no exception. Many of the students come from black Protestant church traditions, and those traditions seep into the college's culture. The students are told that they are not only responsible for individual achievement but also for the collective betterment of their race. If you graduated from Morehouse College, the enrollment process at Strayer University should feel different, if not alien.

"It's different, but it's online. I'll always be a Morehouse Man." Mike did not want or need Strayer to develop his sense of self-worth or identity. Morehouse had done that. So why go to Strayer at all? "You can get in and get out," he said. But the conversation I had overheard suggested that Mike did not have his eye on getting out of Strayer so much as he had his eye on that financial aid refund check. He laughed and said, "This won't be with my name, right?" I assured him that I would anonymize his name and certain facts to protect his identity. "You can get student loan money easy," he explained. He went on to describe a business venture he was planning with four friends, two from Morehouse and the others from his post-graduation days. The business is the sort lauded by entrepreneur incubators and people who give TED talks about the jobs of the future. It was technology based, and between the five of them they had the technical, marketing, and business skills to get it off the ground. He explained it to me. I got the gist. If that's a sign of an idea simple enough to be sold, then it had merit. What the idea didn't have, and what Mike, his partners, and their parents didn't have, was capital. That was where the hustle came in.

If there is a more pervasive opinion about the future of work in the new economy than the need for us all to become entrepreneurs, it is hard to find it. The narrative about entrepreneurship is something like a fairy tale we collectively write to ward off the bad things we cannot name or evade. Work is changing. Young workers like Mike have less job tenure than do older workers. According to the Bureau of Labor Statistics, the median tenure—or time worked for a single employer—for workers between the ages of fifty-five and sixty-four is more than three times that of workers between ages twenty-five and thirty-four. One can hypothesize that as today's young workers get older, they will change jobs less frequently. There are a few reasons not to assume that is true. The service sector holds the greatest share of jobs, and employees in the service sector have the lowest job tenure of all the major occupations. Unless the composition of the job market shifts away from service jobs or service jobs become professionalized, workers will get older but job tenure will remain lower than it was for previous generations of workers. This is one of the arguments of the new-economy research: declining corporate responsibility to workers and the growth of the service sector will mean that workers change jobs more frequently. Mike assumes he will have several employers over his lifetime and that the only path to long job tenure is to not have an employer at all.

Mike may feel that way because, even among those with job ten-ure with just one or two employers for an entire career, a job feels more insecure than it once did. Now Senator Elizabeth Warren and Amelia Warren Tyagi called this the "middle-class squeeze" in their book *The Two-Income Trap*. Hacker calls this the "risk shift." Sociologist Arne Kalleberg, in his book on good jobs and bad jobs, talks about the "hollowed out middle" class jobs.[8] Of course, poor people and the working poor have long felt this squeeze, absorbed this risk, and stared down the gulf between themselves and their dreams. Essentially, even those with good jobs don't feel like those jobs buy the same quality of life as they once did. They are right. Household expenses, education debt, and childcare costs require most people to work more hours just to break even. Increasingly, business gurus and managers suggest that we should always be looking for work so as to keep our resumes sharp and skills up to date. Save at a few employers (i.e., Google) in a handful of in-dustries (i.e., Silicon Valley), most workers are faced with fewer company-sponsored or subsidized benefits that can improve their quality of life. For example, retirement plans were once a corpo-rate benefit of having a "good job," the likes of which one might get after earning a college degree. Hacker shows how corporate contributions to retirement plans have been replaced with indi-vidual retirement accounts in the aggregate, effectively shifting the risk of growing old or sick from employers to workers. The new accounts are said to "empower" workers to control their own money in old age. But the previous plans provided a psychic ben-efit as well as less exposure to the risks inherent to investing in the stock market. To navigate all the risks of working, we're told that we should act like entrepreneurs in our jobs because—the implica-tion suggests—we cannot count on a job to exist even when we have one.

The entrepreneurial worker has a lot of risk to navigate. First, if she goes to college (and research suggests she should, to be viewed as a sound investment risk), an entrepreneurial worker should choose a college and a major with a pipeline to high-reward jobs. Should she get one of those jobs, she should "invest" in herself through continued education and constant networking. LinkedIn has tapped this ethos perfectly. The automated harvesting of every contact one has ever had on almost any social media platform from every aspect of one's life promises to make users invulnerable to risk, or at least less vulnerable. Ideally, the entrepreneurial worker is not only constantly surveying the shifting landscape of one's profession, but is also building a brand, a business on the side, a gig for the gig economy, and, as Mike put it, a hustle. The hustle is like an IRA and a LinkedIn page, a frantic kind of insurance policy that replaces the security of jobs that just don't provide much of it anymore.

Our culture lauds the successful entrepreneurial worker. She may be invited to give a talk about her gig at a TEDx-branded local event. These kinds of events double as networking opportunities to connect with other entrepreneurial workers. The entrepreneurial worker is plugging into a network that can increase her LinkedIn contacts, build her skills, and expand her resume. If she is excessively lucky and plucky, the entrepreneurial worker's side gig becomes an actual business. Perhaps even better, the gig can become a mobile app that disrupts an existing business. Apps and ideas are now regularly funded through a network of private capital arrangements that are exactly like those that funded the expansion of for-profit colleges. If the successful entrepreneurial worker pulls off managing all of this risk, she can extend her brand and sell advice to other entrepreneurial workers hoping to do the same. Beneath the entrepreneurial worker ideal is a complex system of wealth and privilege that people like Mike find themselves navigating. A recent study found that one of the most common traits among "successful" entrepreneurs isn't personality traits or risk-taking behaviors, but family wealth.[9] The jobs of the twenty-first century and the degrees that are often sold as a ticket to them may have a narrative solidly grounded in an imagined future, but the wealth that makes those jobs and degrees real for thousands of people relies on a long history of wealth inequality.

There are three levels to the hustle as Mike described it and as the entrepreneurial worker might experience it. The hustle—the language and the framework—came up time and again in my interviews with current and former for-profit college students. Both men and women, black, white, and Hispanic, all referenced it to some degree, although men used the framework more singularly. Women were more likely to have more than one framework for explaining their educational choices, such as being a good mother as well as executing the hustle. But for most of the students I spoke with, the hustle explained their approach to credentials and job markets.

The first level of the hustle is playing by the rules. The rules, by and large, include graduating high school, going to college, and minimizing any life choices that would impede either (e.g., having a child, running afoul of the criminal justice system). The second level of the hustle is parlaying one's success at following the rules into a job, and once in that job, demonstrating all the right entrepreneurial worker activities (i.e., networking, additional training). The third level of the hustle involves actual entrepreneurialism; traditionally, that has meant starting a business. Mike laid down a hustle ethic that does all three, simultaneously and successfully. He had gone to a good college. While in college, Mike had built relationships with the children of the black elite. He had upgraded the social norms inherited from his lower-middle-class family to include things like international travel and marriage norms. He would marry by age forty, he told me, to a woman who is "about something"; i.e., also hustling. Like many men of his social class, Mike considered marriage and family formation an important life stage, a way to signal his maturation. But his social class—his tastes, preferences, and lifestyle—did not exactly match his economic resources.

Like many African American men, Mike was struggling to meet the dominant culture's expectations of him given the

racialized context of low wages, little inherited family wealth, and
the lower returns to educational attainment that are common for
African Americans in the United States.[10] Like many similarly
positioned African Americans, Mike had developed his side gig
based on some of those college connections. He was networking
in his job at an area utility company and had developed other contacts as well. He networked as a member of organizations like 100
Black Men of Atlanta and a black Greek fraternity. Mike gathered
from all of his networking that he might be better received if he
had a graduate degree. "You have to have those letters after your
name," Mike said. It would not be the first time I heard the idea of
credential inflation or the hustle described that way.

Having letters after one's name had become increasingly important, according to Mike. Some of the networking events he
attended were also community service events. The 100 Black
Men organization might, for example, host a public forum for
young black men with college aspirations. Mike would participate to talk about college and the hustle, and especially to
talk about Morehouse. At these events, participants' name tags
would include an alphabet string: JD, MBA, MD, PhD, EdD,
PsyD, PharmD. For Mike, the letters after a name were signs of
cultural capital.[11] Perhaps more important, they were a sign of
changing norms in a cultural milieu—the black, upwardly mobile, upper-middle class—in which he had invested a great deal
of time and energy adopting as his own. Getting a graduate degree in a field or program that conferred skills as well as a professional designation ("letters") was Mike's initial motivation for
enrolling in an MBA program. This motivation created intersections between Mike's background, aspirations, and resources
that are hard to disentangle. But that really only explains why
Mike would pursue a graduate degree and the type of degree he
sought. It does not explain why Mike would pursue an MBA at
for-profit Strayer. That choice would introduce another set of
intersections—race, wealth, and class—that characterizes how

the entrepreneurial-worker ideal shapes different choices for different groups of people.

You need money to be an entrepreneur. Some people like to pretend that you do not. There is always a story about someone who started with nothing and built an empire. But for some people, "nothing" would be an improvement. Less than nothing means debts or deficits that one must overcome before they break even at nothing. The third level of the hustle—indeed, perhaps its greatest expression—is to become an entrepreneur. Mike had received this message from his peers, his mentors, and the greater culture, and he was all in. What Mike was not, however, was wealthy. He isn't alone. There are more non-wealthy people in the United States than there are wealthy people. Students enrolled in for-profit colleges are more likely to be poor than are students in traditional colleges. We do not have good data on those students' wealth positions, broadly defined to include inheritances of various kinds, but it is safe to say that some of the characteristics found among for-profit students suggest that they aren't in line for a trust fund. They tend to have a higher number of unmet needs, which qualifies them for more student aid, for example. They are also disproportionately non-white, with one in seven of all black students in higher education being enrolled in a for-profit college compared with one in twelve among all college students.

Also important is what race has got to do with wealth. As it turns out, a great deal. In 2013, white households had thirteen times the median wealth of black households.[12] You might think, given the history of racist discrimination that has prevented blacks from entering and benefiting from the kinds of arrangements that build wealth—education, jobs, housing—that this is better than it used to be. Depending on your starting point, you would be wrong. In 2010, white households had eight times the median wealth of black households. Black–white and Hispanic–white wealth disparities are approaching (and in some cases exceeding) the historical highs seen just after the civil rights movement. The

Demos Foundation reminds us that wealth inequalities don't fall from the sky; they are the expected outcomes of persistent public policy choices that maintain white wealth advantages over black wealth accrual.[13] Blacks and Latinos save, buy homes, and value wealth as much as whites do, but they see much lower returns on the single greatest wealth-building vehicle for Americans: their homes. Demos says this is mostly due to policies like redlining, which reinforced racial residential segregation. The poorest whites in the United States have slightly more wealth than blacks who qualify as having a middle income.[14] How important is wealth to entrepreneurship, that great achievement of the modern worker? Summing up the research, Andrew Oswald says that "entrepreneurship is more about cash than dash" or risk-taking ambitions.[15] "If one does not have money in the form of a family with money, the chances of becoming an entrepreneur drop quite a bit," according to Ross Levine, whose study on wealth and entrepreneurship shows that traits common among entrepreneurs include being white, male, and well educated.

Mike's risk-taking ambitions had driven him to choose graduate school, even when he would rather not ("I'm tired of school"). His place in a long historical narrative about racism and wealth inequality was part of what drove him to choose Strayer and not a "real" college: "The financial aid is easy," he said. Why is the financial aid so easy or accessible and straightforward when compared to the financial aid at local traditional colleges, many of which offer less-expensive MBAs with course flexibility and even online options? After all, it is the same pot of federal money being accessed using the same Free Application for Federal Student Aid (FAFSA). According to Mike, the financial aid process at Strayer was qualitatively different. It was faster and easier. The financial aid officer was "nice" and handled many of the details that used to hang Mike up at Morehouse. We shared a joke about standing in long lines at our respective historically black colleges to straighten out our financial aid paperwork. The reality is that many colleges have complex bureaucracies that make it difficult for students to access and process their financial aid. After four and a half years of navigating the financial aid office at Morehouse, the Strayer process was a relief: a single point of contact, direct assistance completing paperwork, and few hiccups in getting his student loan refund. In many ways, because Mike had experience with traditional higher education, he was *more* amenable to the for-profit college's streamlined process and not turned off by it, as many people would and do assume.

Not only was the financial aid process at Strayer easier than the one Mike remembered from undergrad, but it was also a low-risk path to capital that Mike needed to meet his entrepreneurial goals. Unfortunately for Mike, he had not seen to being born white, male, and wealthy, as research would suggest he be in order to be successful in the entrepreneur ecosystem. But two generations of black middle-class mobility had exposed Mike to a culture of entrepreneurial workers, a.k.a. the hustle, which required capital unlikely to come easily to the children of the black middle class. In 2012, Mike was not in an economic climate that was friendly for those who want capital and do not already have any. Easy credit had precipitated the Great Recession. Securitized credit (things like mortgage-backed securities) had made money for those with capital to invest, but had drained the housing value of those who did not have capital.[16] And for those *really* without—African Americans and Hispanics—the recession had disproportionately decimated entire housing communities and credit profiles and rolled back one to three generations of wealth building.

Today's credit market is for both prime consumers and subprime consumers, which sounds cliché. The two groups have long existed as distinct markets made up of people with very different relationships to credit and money, and to jobs and education. But there had been, for a moment after the 1980s and before the 2008 crash, a middle market. It was a market space between check-cashing joints and wealth-management consultants. Ten years earlier, Mike might have maxed out credit cards, maximized his disposable income, or talked his parents into using their home equity line, which they'd earned via a modest house with modest value gains over a few decades. In the 2010s, however, Mike was indeed living off his credit cards, but he had little disposable income after paying for household expenses and the consumption costs of living middle class. And his parents? They were now anything but a fallback plan, since they did not have the equity or wealth to provide him a buffer. When we spoke, Mike said he saw two options for capital: "get a sugar momma" or take out a student loan.

Taking out the student loan would actually be easier than getting a sugar momma, if only because there are far fewer upfront costs. Mike tapped his network of similarly aspirational blacks in the entrepreneurial-worker mold. He realized many of them had earned the letters after their names from colleges he'd never considered, like the one with a location right there in Lenox Mall. A woman who was almost finished with her MBA at Strayer offered Mike her coursework. The classes were all online. Therefore, there was virtually no risk in recycling the work in online discussion boards and for assignments submitted to professors who frequently changed. Remember from Chapter 1 that for-profit colleges maximize profit margins by using centralized, standardized curriculums. They also manage costs by minimizing the number of full-time faculty. That means students like Mike and the woman who offered him the finished coursework could be fairly certain the assignments would be the same even if the course was taught by a different professor. This minimized Mike's opportunity costs—the lost wages, time, or resources he might earn were he not going back to college.

"[In] one year, you can stack about seven or eight thousand dollars" from financial aid loans, Mike said. It wasn't much, but it was a lump sum not tied to his housing or transportation. Consequently, should he have trouble repaying the loans, his car wouldn't be repossessed and his home (if he had one; Mike was renting) would not be foreclosed upon. No doubt there are risks to defaulting on student loans. One's wages and tax refunds can be garnished. One's credit profile can be destroyed. But those are risks that the poor, near poor, and working poor absorb every day even without student loans. It was a competing narrative someone like Mike inherited from his black working-class roots, and it would condition how he viewed risks in his upwardly mobile, black, middle-class present. Mike never talked about institutional prestige. "Good" schools, college rankings, and perceptions of degree status were not foreign concepts to Mike. Still, the college calculus based on prestige wasn't the only life math he knew. He also knew about debt and wasn't afraid of it. He knew about inequalities in opportunities and resources, like small business loans or private equity investment. He also knew that when the name tag at the community service event lists the letters after your name, it rarely lists the institution that granted them.

Of the two streams of the Lower Ed river, Mike would be in the calmer waters. He is, by all objective measures that we use to determine such things, an education success story. He may be considered successful even more so given the salient narrative about black men's poor educational attainment and mobility. He has a degree from a good school with a brand name. He has embraced the current iteration of the capitalist work ethic with its entrepreneurial-worker ethos. He has translated that ethos into culturally relevant terms—the hustle—and is working it on all three levels.[17] But at each level Mike bumps up against inequalities. He has played by the rules, but at a cost that the wealthy rarely have to pay.

Mike has student loans from undergrad, as do over 94 percent of black college students, compared with 69 percent of white students. He attended one of the 107 historically black colleges, which categorically have fewer institutional resources than do predominately white colleges and universities to help offset Mike's need for student loan money. Black colleges have been blatantly and systematically underfunded using public policies similar to those that create racial wealth disparities.[18] As a result, HBCUs often have small endowments to help students who are more likely to have greater financial needs. College and university endowments are a form of institutional wealth. Generally, endowments are used to manage long-term investments in the college, like funds to support research. However, when other forms of revenue are down or operating costs increase, universities can increase their spending to "help moderate higher tuition increases, maintain or increase student aid, and support the quality of their programs."[19] When an institution has a smaller endowment it cannot increase spending to offset budget cuts, for example. This leaves institutions in the position of HBCUs with few choices during difficult times. They can increase tuition, decrease aid, or compromise curriculum quality.

Despite the risks, Mike executes the second level of the hustle, building up his networks and vigilantly cultivating his brand. He was at Lenox Mall that day to "invest" in new clothes that present Mike, The Professional™ in the best way possible to potential connections. He sat down with me, in part, because my card had a university brand attached, and in Atlanta you never know when a black person might be one of the black elite. It's best to err on the side of entertaining random strangers who eavesdrop on your conversations when you've got an eye on the entrepreneurial hustle. Finally, Mike chose Strayer because its processes were transparent, making them easy to hustle. He could count on easy access to financial aid refunds and an online class structure with an underground economy of coursework that could be bought or borrowed. Each of these characteristics lowered the risk of enrollment for Mike by means that a traditional college was unlikely to offer. And each of these decision points was as much about our socioeconomic condition as it was about Strayer University. Even under the best of circumstances, with as few risk factors as possible for dropping out or defaulting, Mike's experience at the top of the for-profit college food chain was still marked by inequalities.

When even the best of times is a sign of some pretty bad times, the success of for-profit colleges is evidence of large systemic failures well outside the universe of higher education.

Mike is one of the thousands of people enrolled in the second-fastest-growing subsector of for-profit colleges: graduate or post-baccalaureate programs.[20] Recall from the previous chapter that I analyzed all of the documents that publicly traded for-profit colleges (the largest and most dominant among the sector) filed with the SEC. As early as the late 1990s, the for-profit college sector had an eye on people like Mike, a working adult. Grand Canyon said that working adults are "an attractive student population because they are better able to finance their education, more readily recognize the benefits of a postsecondary degree, and have higher persistence and completion rates than students generally." Working adults like Mike also promise a longer revenue stream as they seek "graduate degrees to obtain pay increases or job promotions that are directly tied to higher educational attainment." More Mikes has meant a shift in the composition of the for-profit college universe. Even as news abounds of chains closing and declining enrollments, for-profit colleges have, for at least ten years, been shifting focus to programs with less risk. These programs are more likely to offer some letters after one's name. By shifting resources to graduate programs, for-profit colleges have reduced a major cost (new curriculum development) and maximized the profit from better-prepared students more likely to graduate (graduate students) and less likely to endanger an institution's job placement statistics (many graduate students are already employed and/or are less likely to be unemployed after graduation[21]).

Wandering Through the (Education) Desert

Even with the growth in the number of graduate degrees offered, the majority of for-profit college students are seeking their first degree. They are not Mikes. They are Londons. London is forty-eight years old, and I met her through a family friend. A colleague once joked that black academics are more likely to know someone in the criminal justice system than are white academics because of the intricate institutional racism that Michelle Alexander describes in painstaking detail in *The New Jim Crow*. No matter how far the social distance between poor blacks and wealthy blacks, social problems like police violence truncate the road between us. For-profit colleges are similar. I field calls and emails all the time from black academics with a sister, a mother, or a cousin enrolled in a for-profit college. They wonder if the school is legitimate. They worry that their loved one is being scammed. They are ashamed or inclined not to air their dirty laundry with white colleagues or on public forums like social media. They pull me aside at conferences or send me a note begging my forgiveness or send me a private message on Twitter. They send me messages about loved ones that, were it not for my experiences and research, I myself could have written.

London is one of five people in my circle of intimates who is or has been enrolled in a for-profit college. They run the gamut from certificate programs at Everest College to MBAs at Capella University. I have known London for over a decade in the way you know someone through phone conversations with your mother in which she catches you up on people you vaguely remember. London is a mother of three, and her oldest is sixteen years younger than she is. Like the majority of the female students in for-profit colleges, London is a primary caregiver and is enrolled in a certificate program. She has enrolled in some kind of post–high school program at least five times in the years that I have known her. She has finished one short-term certificate program before. When Corinthian Colleges began its documented implosion in 2014, London was still posting happy pictures of herself at school with her friends. She had no idea that her college had just been forced into closure (which would later become a phased buyout that remains in flux at the time of this writing).

More than Mike—male, traditionally degreed, single, and childless—London is who many of us think of when we think about people who attend for-profit colleges. The research here is clear, if sometimes insulting. For-profit colleges are said to be either "predators" or "nimble critters" in how they effectively recruit (if not graduate) millions of students considered to be "low status." Low-status students may not have been pegged for any traditional college pathway because they are older (than, say, twenty-four years of age) or are parents with dependent children (especially if they are mothers and heads of household; i.e., the dreaded single mother). Even if they do not have children, they may be place-bound because culture or commitment dictates that they take care of a parent or a cousin or younger siblings. They may have a general equivalency degree (GED) as opposed to a traditional high school diploma. Even if they have a high school diploma, they probably took basic math instead of calculus, a second English class instead of a foreign language. Because of this, even if they aspire to college, they may find themselves with a high school diploma that does not meet or exceed the minimum admissions requirements at their state's university system.[22] They may decide to go to the military instead of college. Or, as the military has dramatically reduced in size, these would-be students may find themselves looking for work instead of filling out college applications. For myriad reasons, students in the for-profit college sector's rockier stream are likely to be labeled "non-traditional," like London.

London has gone to school every time her life has become untenable. When she was a seventeen-year-old new mother, London took a computer certification class. She stopped going when she found a job working nights. Her mother worked days. Between the two of them, they did not have to pay for childcare costs for the baby. That worked until London fell in love. She wanted what many people want for their children but that not everyone has the means to provide—stability. Marriage struck her as a solution on many fronts. First, it would prove to those in her immediate family that she was not "somebody's baby momma," as she told me. For black women in particular, the stigma of being good enough to be a mother but not good enough to be a wife can seem to confirm society's assumptions that one's life is over when you have a child. "I love my baby. I'm glad I had her young," London says.[23] What she didn't exactly love was the censure from her religious aunts and the cousins who seemed to be "doing things the right way": going to college, marrying before having children, buying cars, and setting up households.

London knew Leon from high school. They reconnected after London and her daughter's father separated. Leon had a good job for a place like the rural North Carolina town in which they lived. The small town was built by the textile industry. Everything about the town retains the culture of mills, manufacturing, and manual labor. The race and class distinctions in such a place are not just deeply interwoven; their gradation is so subtle as to require full cultural immersion to parse them. In a larger town with more diverse, modern industries, a mobile trailer home can mark a person and place as poor. Where London and Leon were from, a trailer on wheels might be poor, but a trailer with a cinder-block foundation was solidly working class. A modular home or small brick rancher on some land, and not in a planned community development, is middle class. Rich and wealthy do not really operate here as terms. There are people with "family money," like those who once owned a large chair-making operation and now run an artisan craft shop. But you do not work your way up to family money like Mike worked his way into Atlanta's black elite. In London's hometown you aspire to a middle-class rancher, thank God for a working-class cinder-block foundation, and make do with a trailer on wheels.

There are two traditional post-secondary institutions where London lives. The University is a small, private college with bucolic grounds that boasts about its "24/7 residential learning experience." The student population is not prey for nimble critters and predators. They come from across the state, and in 2012 almost a fourth of them came from out of state. The Community College is three times the size of the University. Given its local dominance, the Community College often has waiting lists for popular programs. Consequently, London says it has been known to turn away students who are not academically prepared for the coursework. London's town is not New York or D.C. or Atlanta, or even Cleveland or Santa Fe. Midsized and large urban cores so dominate our collective imagination that it is easy to overlook the hundreds of what education researchers Nicholas Hillman and Taylor Weichman of the University of Wisconsin-Madison have called "education deserts."[24] These are cities, towns, *spaces* across the country where there are few college options (and effectively no options for students who are not like London). As Hillman and Weichman argue, for many students "shopping around" is an oxymoron. As for London, proximity can be higher education destiny. There are more traditional college options forty to sixty miles away, but that requires a car that is up for that kind of regular abuse and the money to make the trip for months or years on end. For London, this landscape means that other than her first foray into a computer certificate program in the early 1990s, she has always attended a for-profit program when she drops back into school as her life demands.

When we sat down formally to talk about life and school and work in 2011, London had just used her tax refund to repay a defaulted student loan. She had owed a little more than $4,000 for a stint at Brookstone College of Business.[25] Brookstone is like the hundreds of for-profit colleges that aren't like the University of Phoenix. They are mostly small, local, and regional chains that specialize in certificates and associate's degrees. They usually concentrate in allied health (e.g., medical records) and "business" courses, the modern iteration of what were once called secretarial

programs. Like the Beauty College, these schools are often family owned and operated. Some went on buying sprees during the
Wall Street era, consolidating smaller schools. But many, like
Brookstone and hundreds of others across the country, remain
small and narrowly focused. There are so many of these schools,
with such diverse operational practices, that one research study
estimates we undercount the total for-profit college universe by
thousands.[26] In education deserts where the practical options are
few, these for-profit schools became a way of life for people like
London. She knew Brookstone's name just as well as she knew the
local university's, if not better. The name recognition mattered
each time London decided to go back to school "to get [herself]
together."

On one such quest, London was recovering from her husband's
early death. She now had three children and seven grandchildren,
with various configurations relying upon her at different times
for numerous forms of support. She now had a home out on some
land thanks to Leon's benefits and a small amount of money left
to her when her grandmother died. London had been enrolled in
Brookstone when Leon fell ill. She stopped going and never officially withdrew. Had she done so, London might have saved a
few hundred dollars in tuition owed, but those are the kinds of details that get lost in complicated lives. The student loan of "about
$2,400" fell through the same cracks as the withdrawal deadlines
did. By the time London came up for air, the small student loan
was in default. In this way, London is typical of those who default
on student loans. Despite all of the media interest in high student
debt–load stories, the students most likely to default on their student loans owe closer to London's $2,400 than Mike's expected
$60,000 in total student debt. The probability of defaulting on
a student loan actually isn't correlated with how much a student
owes.[27] Instead, default seems to be highest among those who do
not earn the credentials and were struggling with debt payments
before they even took on the student loan. Basically, people who

were already suffering from inequalities in wealth, income, and re-sources default on student loans that, by objective measures, are quite small. This pattern makes student loan defaults an inequality problem rather than a financing-scheme problem. The small debts cut deepest because the poorest students take them on. What we know about poverty and near-poverty is that small sums of cash can derail months of careful planning and a year's worth of ambitions. Debt is not absolute but relative—relative to how far below nothing you were when you took the debt on and how close to breaking even you are when it's time to repay it.

London might have repaid her defaulted loan "the bootleg way" earlier by letting the student loan servicer garnish her IRS refund. However, that year she didn't have a refund for them to claim. The largesse of earned income tax credits (EITC), said to help bolster the working poor, relies on one *working*. As Leon was dying, London worked plenty, but being an unpaid caretaker is not the kind of work that earns one a tax credit.

It took London three years to pay off the defaulted student loan and become eligible for another. By that time, she had, over the course of her life, tried various programs in computers ("fixing networks"), electronics ("it was … I'm not sure what that was!"), childcare ("to start my own business and stay home with the babies"), and medical billing ("you have to memorize all these codes"). When we talked, she was enrolled in a medical assistant certificate program. On its website, Everest College says, "Medical assistant is Everest's most popular career training program." The enrollment counselor at London's branch of Everest College said she would be well suited for the career because "I'm a people person. I am always smiling. You know me." Everest also says that the "healthcare industry" is projected to grow "faster than average" into 2025, making it a sure bet for people like London who are "tired of working these [dead-end] jobs." Everest describes a "medical assistant" as being valuable support in a community of credentialed professionals like doctors and nurses. The implication is that London, all the Londons, will be similarly credentialed and professional when they finish the medical assistant program. For sure, London believes her lifetime of low-wage jobs with volatile work schedules would be over if she could get an "office job," one that signals inclusion in a community of workers who take hour lunches and don't work weekends and have plastic health insurance ID cards in their wallets.

London is betting on entering the fastest-growing and thus most secure sector of the labor market: healthcare. She will pay approximately $24,000 for a certificate for an unlicensed job that includes "greeting patients" and "completing health questionnaires." The median pay for a medical assistant in 2014 was $29,370 a year. In London's hometown, with its abandoned textiles and reliance on service sector jobs, that salary would put her within a stone's throw of the area's median salary of $31,924. She hopes the occupation is growing fast enough to get her over the hump of experience needed. Of 102 job ads analyzed in 2015 for a medical assistant within 25 miles of London's home, all but two required one to three years' clinical experience. Some of those jobs required specific training in various medical specialties, like cardiology, radiology, and pediatrics. London says her training at Everest doesn't include a medical specialty, but it does offer her experience in a "clinical setting." I ask her about her backup plan. After a moment she smiles and says, "Jesus! Jesus is my backup plan."

Selling Dreams and Insurance

In both public lectures and emails, I get two questions more than any other: "Why do people go to 'those' schools?" and "What about accreditation?" I deal with accreditation in other chapters. The question of why people go to "those" schools is a good one. It is not a good question because it is particularly elegant, however. It is actually a pretty clunky and complicated question, especially for a sociologist. What people? What do you mean by "those" schools? Why is this abnormal? What is the normal way to go to a school? What is a normal school? See, it's not as simple as it sounds. (Trust me, the accreditation question is even clunkier.) Yet the question is good *because* it is so clunky, so laden with embedded assumptions, anxieties, and projections.

Let us begin with what research says. Research about for-profit colleges tends to ebb and flow with the sector's boom–scandal–bust cycle. Professor Kevin Kinser points out that there's a long history of research conducted on for-profit colleges, but rarely does it constitute a cohesive body of research. That's mostly because researchers "rediscover" the sector when there is public interest or a new federal data set to play with. Then they quickly move on to more sustainable research agendas. It isn't hard to study for-profit colleges, per se. But it is hard to study the most complex and interesting parts of how and why for-profit colleges exist and why millions of people attend them. It is difficult to study for three reasons.

First, for-profit colleges move faster than traditional colleges. People like economist Richard Vedder say that for-profit colleges are leaner, meaner organizations. Researcher William Tierney says that for-profit colleges are more responsive to changing tastes in student markets because they are more nimble. That nimbleness means that schools shutter, new campuses are started, and programs morph with speeds that few traditional not-for-profit colleges can match. Our systems for collecting data on colleges and our methods for studying education are very much designed for slower-moving targets.

Second, for-profit colleges have to comply with various state, federal, and accreditation agencies' practices (the "triad" of higher education regulation). Consequently, they produce a lot of data points so as to remain legal entities. However, this isn't particularly useful data for the kinds of questions embedded in "why do people go to these schools?" Various researchers have parsed those data in almost as many ways as is possible for what those data can answer. They can tell us things like the demographics of who attends for-profit colleges, how many students are enrolled, and the basics of programs and tuition costs. Those data cannot tell us exactly how many students are enrolled in for-profit colleges, because not all for-profit colleges have to report to the same single entity. For example, that beauty school in Charlotte where I once got my hair done by aspiring students? It does not have to report certain data to accreditation agencies if it does not seek accreditation. Schools that pursue accreditation usually do so because they need to be accredited to participate in federal student aid programs. If you do not want to offer federal grants and loans and prefer to deal with students who are self-financing their tuition, there will be little data available on your institution. For that reason, the data we have can best describe the large for-profit colleges, which are likely large because they participate in federal student aid programs.

Finally, the questions we ask about *these* students and *those* schools are questions that benefit from direct access to students, longitudinal data, and sustained research agendas. Why do we know so much about students in traditional colleges? Because most academic researchers work in traditional colleges. Researchers that have an imperative—financial or normative—to produce research have a pool of subjects available to them just beyond their office doors. To complement the quantitative data that places like the Department of Education collect, we have traditionally done smaller studies in our little corners of traditional higher education. What is the analog in the for-profit college sector?

One of the for-profit colleges' great disruptions is to the role of faculty, who are rarely expected to be active researchers.[28] Research in for-profit colleges is more likely to fall under "marketing" as opposed to "academics." Consequently, that research is proprietary, and releasing it as traditional academics do for public vetting is seen as a risk to market competitiveness. For-profit colleges certainly conduct the research to answer the questions traditional research cannot or will not answer (why these students, at these schools, to what unequal ends). But they have absolutely no market-based incentive to publish that data or act in the interest of knowledge production when it is in conflict with profit taking. Beyond the mandates of the market, when the goal is how to better identify and recruit new students (as opposed to understanding the achievement differences between students, as a sociologist might study), the for-profit college market-research apparatus is sophisticated and devastating in its precision. To explore the difference data could make, it is helpful to start with a summary of what we presently know in the realm of research and then compare it to what for-profit colleges know.

There are rough estimates of how many students are enrolled in for-profit colleges. Official statistics put approximately 1.2 million students in a for-profit college. But that official statistic only accounts for the for-profit colleges that administer federal financial aid. Economists Stephanie Riegg Cellini and Claudia Goldin used data from state and federal sources to estimate the real enrollment in for-profit colleges at 2.4 million students. It is fair to say that there were between one and two million students enrolled in a for-profit college as of 2010. We have a good sense of what programs and degrees for-profit colleges offer. There is more program diversity among those schools that offer federal financial aid, ranging from certificates to PhDs and JDs (almost everything but an MD). There is less diversity among schools that don't offer financial aid: most of them offer certificates and associate's degrees.[29] In 2009, the for-profit colleges tracked by the Department of Education conferred 42 percent of vocational certificates, 18 percent of associate's degrees, 5 percent of bachelor's degrees, and 10 percent of master's degrees awarded overall. We know for-profit colleges can be expensive for students. The oft-quoted statistic is from a multiyear Senate investigation of thirty for-profit colleges, released in 2012: "on average, BA programs cost 19% more than at flagship public universities, associate's degree programs four times more than at community colleges, and certificate programs cost four times more than at community colleges."[30] Over 94 percent of students enrolled in for-profit colleges that participate in federal financial aid programs use those programs to pay their tuition. As a result, looking at their debt burdens might give us a more precise view of the costs students pay at for-profit colleges.

A 2014 report from The Institute for College Access and Success (TICAS) puts some of the debt numbers in context.[31] Debt burdens for all college students are increasing, and that is just as true for those in for-profit colleges. Average debt levels for all graduating seniors with student loans rose to $29,400 in 2012—a 25 percent increase from $23,450 in 2008. For those in for-profit colleges, average debt was $39,950, twenty-six percent higher than in 2008, when the average was $31,800. I once presented similar figures at an academic conference. A senior academic blithely replied, "So basically this so-called crushing 'debt' is the price of a mid-sized, mid-market sedan." He was right. Forty grand will buy you a Honda. But he was also making a common mistake: debt is not absolute. As we learned from Mike and London both, it is relative. Forty thousand dollars in debt when you begin with family wealth or when you can determine that you'll likely have a high-earning job for a long period of time makes forty grand look like peanuts. It is why almost no one talks about the extreme amount of debt that, say, a law student at Harvard will take on, even though the average graduate in 2015 carried $149,754 in student loan debt. Because they're at Harvard and they'll be Harvard-educated lawyers, this large debt isn't considered a travesty. But even a $5,000 debt is onerous when your net worth is negative and your expected job prospects are low. One woman's Honda is another man's Mercedes.

Understanding the difference between absolute debt numbers—fifty dollars or five hundred dollars or fifty thousand dollars—and relative debt—for instance, choosing which bill will be paid because you cannot pay them all—gets at the heart of how inequality shows up at for-profit colleges. Let's recall the demographics of for-profit college students. Despite being the smallest sector of higher education, more low-income black and Hispanic women were enrolled in for-profit colleges than in four-year public and private colleges combined in 2008.[32] Only 75 percent of students in for-profit colleges have a high school diploma. The rest have general equivalency diplomas and other non-traditional high school certifications. And they're more likely to be quite poor, with 16 percent of for-profit students participating in a welfare program as compared with 2.6 percent in traditional colleges.[33]

Data on the day-to-day experiences of inequality, poverty, sexism, and racism among students in for-profit colleges are slim to none. But that's precisely the data that answers questions like the one that vexes so many people: Why do students go to *those* schools? There is a tendency among researchers to say there is something inherently inferior about the students themselves: they have low cognitive functioning and ipso facto enroll in schools with little selection criteria.[34] On the other end of the spectrum, researchers do not investigate what being black or poor means for the experience of debt, choice, and inequality. Rather, they take it as a natural starting point for understanding the inherent differences among people.[35] These sound like opposing viewpoints, but they share the same assumptions: that something inherent to being black or Hispanic or female would make the decision to enroll in a for-profit college perfectly rational.

To revisit the primary theme of this book, what if the choices aren't about who students are, but rather are about what makes certain choices available to some people at the expense of others? That is what I saw at the Beauty College and the Technical College. It is what students time and again have explained to me. And it is what for-profit college actors know very well—a lot has to happen to make a choice seem rational. The students at the Beauty College faced different obstacles to starting and staying in school. The Beauty College had created a system of marketing and enrolling that matched those students' obstacles. Those obstacles were similar in some ways but different in other ways than the ones students at the Technical College faced. The Technical College's different marketing and enrollment reflected those distinctions. The choices felt rational when the right for-profit college aligned with the right kinds of obstacles and the students who have them in common. We sold dreams—of mobility, stability, and status—to students at the Beauty College. At the Technical College, we sold insurance—policies against unemployment, career stagnation, and volatile job markets. The latter was actually the more privileged position. Those students largely had jobs. They more often had the money for application fees. They came with their parents more frequently. They were dealing with inequalities, but of a different character and severity than those confronting the students at the Beauty College. That for-profit colleges have figured out how to enroll both groups of students, and how to make their choice to enroll seem rational, speaks to why the sector expanded 225 percent in the first decade of the twenty-first century.

I enrolled eight students my first week at the Beauty College. The office had been understaffed for some time, which created pent-up demand. My second week on the job I met Clarice. It would be almost a year before she started the program. The delay had little to do with her commitment or cognitive functioning or any other inherent fixed characteristics. Like the others, she did not need much convincing to set up an appointment or to eventually sign the enrollment paperwork. It took Clarice almost a year to start a program that she could have finished in that time because being working poor and black and a mother means something in our society. What those things mean made the Beauty College a rational choice in the way that dousing your burning leg with cold water is rational: it helps but you are still scarred.

Clarice was in her early twenties but looked like a teenager. When I called her, she told me that she had a car and knew how to get to the school. Those were always two of the biggest obstacles to setting up an appointment at the Beauty College. Clarice was motivated and had cleared the first two hurdles easily enough. But then she didn't show for her appointment. As was standard operating procedure, I called her to "gauge her interest and motivation." No one wanted to keep that appointment more than Clarice. She was audibly upset about possibly making me angry. She kept apologizing for missing the appointment (although she didn't quite connect it to not calling to tell me that she would miss it). When we finally met face to face, Clarice was very quiet. She was so quiet and asked so few questions that I assumed that she wasn't interested in enrolling. I offered her a chance to enroll only because my training dictated that I should and not because I thought she would. I was surprised when she immediately nodded and sat up straight to sign the enrollment paperwork. I realized she had been quiet because for her enrolling was a foregone conclusion. It was as if she'd entertained my spiel, but could have skipped it altogether. Clarice signed on the dotted line with no problem. My next step in the process was to give her a copy of the FAFSA. The FAFSA is the only means of applying for and receiving the "grants and loans" promised in the Beauty College's commercials. The form asks for wage and income information, the kind of information typically found on your end-of-year wage statements from an employer and filed with the Internal Revenue Service (IRS) at tax time.

The FAFSA caused my students at the Beauty College a lot of angst. This was less true for students at the Technical College. Like Clarice, students at the Beauty College often had only negative financial relationships on which to base their understanding of financial aid. Clarice froze when I handed her the form and asked her to set up her next appointment to go over it. Noticing her body language, I prodded for the reason. Eventually, Clarice got around to voicing her fear: could her student loan be rejected for having bad credit? I explained by answering the question based on the differences between federal student loans (no), parent loans (yes), and private student loans (yes). Clarice was visibly relieved.

It would still take us weeks to complete her FAFSA, however. The problems with getting it completed were related to the pressures under which my students typically found themselves.

First, Clarice could not negotiate the tax forms away from their location in her mother's house. Clarice had a tumultuous relationship with her mother, something not nearly as atypical as our federal student aid system assumes. I had students whose parents supported their aspirations but flatly refused to share their tax information to complete the FAFSA when a parent's information was required. The reasons for refusing ranged from intra-family conflict to fears about immigration status to distrust of any kind of financial arrangement. Clarice didn't need her mother's consent, because Clarice had a son. She was considered "independent" of her parents by virtue of her own parental status. But Clarice needed to navigate fraught emotional terrain to get the forms from her mother's house. Clarice also could not provide documentation of her citizenship status. We needed a birth certificate or a passport. I can only recall one student at the Beauty College ever having a passport for these purposes. Almost all of the students brought in birth certificates. Clarice did not have hers. Clarice's mother couldn't provide it. Clarice needed to go to the vital records office to get her birth certificate.

For weeks, I called and followed up with Clarice about the birth certificate. She had been born one state over in South Carolina. Fortunately, Charlotte sits right at the state line. The fifteen-minute drive across state lines was actually more convenient than the drive across town to the North Carolina office. Clarice had access to the car. What was the hold-up? Clarice eventually admitted that she was afraid to go to the records office by herself. The bureaucracy intimidated her. After a few days of pep talks, I gave in and drove her to the vital records office so that she wouldn't be alone. We can debate the merits of someone like Clarice going to college, any college, if she is too shy to speak up in an admissions appointment and too scared to get her birth certificate. But that kind of moralizing is unproductive. The fact is, Clarice exists. A lot of Clarices exist.

Aaron knows that lots of Clarices exist; he had the data to prove it. Unlike the earlier summary of what we know about for-profit colleges and the students enrolled in them, Aaron had a better picture of students' experiences of work, life, and why they choose for-profit colleges. Aaron was in charge of marketing research for a large, national shareholder for-profit college. Aaron found me through my public writing and blogging and social media and decided that speaking to me might be interesting. He emailed me and kept emailing me over the course of a year. Eventually, I was giving a lecture in the same state where he lived, and he invited me to have coffee. Aaron's job in marketing research is a bit misleading. For-profit colleges do not do academic research as an institutional imperative. For-profit colleges with graduate programs, especially those that confer PhDs, have students who do research and faculty that supervise them. But this is not the primary interest. The research in that context is part of conferring the degree, not spurred by the knowledge-creation ethos that legitimizes traditional research universities. For-profit colleges might not do traditional research, the likes of which has produced reams of data on traditional college students, but that does not mean that for-profit colleges don't do research. They do a lot of research. They just have a different purpose: the pursuit of effective marketing, rather than the pursuit of knowledge.

Aaron had undergraduate and graduate degrees from an Ivy League university. He had left finance to work at a for-profit college overseeing market research because he "got tired of working just for the sake of making money." Aaron wanted to make a difference. Like me, but for different reasons, Aaron had come to for-profit colleges knowing only what recruiters had told him about them: they serve the underserved and deserving. He told me that a draft paper I'd shared online with my findings from my study of admissions at for-profit colleges was "spot on," save for one point about the value of a new student as opposed to a returning student (Aaron said a returning student was more cost-effective). I knew what I wanted from Aaron. I was curious about the research machine at for-profit colleges and the worldview of those high up that food chain. I wasn't sure what Aaron wanted from me.

Over coffee, it turned out that Aaron wanted to figure out why he thought he was helping students but couldn't shake the feeling that he wasn't. "I don't think community colleges do a demonstrably better job serving our students than we do," he said. Depending on how one measures "better," Aaron was right. "Our students get solid training for the workforce. We're beefing up what we call their 'soft skills' because that's the number one reason they do not get a call back from a potential employer. They don't know how to handle themselves in an interview—they bring their kids or they're late or what have you. We're working on that." I was struck by Aaron's confident summation of why their students struggle to enter the labor market. None of the academic research on for-profit colleges has good answers for the questions about why for-profit students do or do not fare well in the labor market. Indeed, despite the deeply held assumption among many and the very public debates about job-placement data, there isn't even consensus that for-profit students fare poorly in what we call labor market returns. By returns I mean the likelihood of being employed (or unemployed), for how long, at what time, and in what kind of occupation.

Publicly accessible data on the labor market outcomes of for-profit college students relies on the for-profit colleges to report that data. Some question that data's veracity given that for-profit colleges are always under the threat of losing access to student aid if those numbers are compromised. It is also true that some for-profit colleges have been found guilty of fudging the numbers. For example, one investigation of a career college in 2008 found that the for-profit college had paid local employers to "hire" students. That could be fine in the grand scheme of placing students in jobs (like a very crude paid internship of sorts), except this school had structured the job to end after six months, just long enough for the student to be counted as employed for federal data purposes, and they did so without telling the student that the job was temporary.

The available data on for-profit colleges' job-placement rate is also hampered by the politics that accompany all educational data in the United States. We have several systems for tracking student data. The Department of Education's system collects data only on students who receive federal financial aid. The IRS captures data on people who use the education tax credit or deduct their student loan interest. The Department of Veteran's Affairs tracks the students who use their GI benefits and educational programs. And some states have a single database for in-state students. None of these systems talk to each other. Consequently, students can be reported to numerous databases simultaneously, and researchers can't do any checks for duplication or errors. Attempts at a coordinated system for observing how students enroll, borrow, progress, graduate, and work ended in 2008 when an amendment to the Higher Education Act's reauthorization banned agencies from connecting individual-level data.

Thus, the best data we have on students in for-profit colleges relies either on the accuracy of the schools' self-reports or on a snapshot of students enrolled at any one time. Snapshots could be the same students as were in that school the year prior or could be an entirely different group of students, with different characteristics. This is a real problem if you want to determine, for instance, whether students with the same race, class, gender, and high school training will enter the labor market with a good job compared with similar students in a traditional college. For researchers, this means using the data we have very creatively, which is also a surefire way to inherit a lot of problems in your analysis. With Aaron, I hit the jackpot. His confident assertion said he not only knew how individual students (at the large for-profit college where he worked) did when they tried to get a job, but he also knew the contextual reasons for why they did or did not get jobs. I was obviously curious as to how they knew so much about their students given how little researchers were able to figure out about those same students.

Aaron described a complex (and enviable) research apparatus at his for-profit college. That research apparatus revealed how for-profit colleges like his—national, shareholder, primarily certificate and associate granting—are organized to recruit the millions of students that generate billions of dollars in profit. How they do that is clearly about "the types of students we serve," as Aaron frequently put it. That is, the systems are about the inequalities that some students show up with when they *call now.* "We spend a lot of money finding our students. Our kind of students are hard to find," Aaron explained. His for-profit college employed a small army of workers who would go door to door at students' last-known addresses and the addresses of the family and friends students had listed on their enrollment paperwork. These door-knockers are important to the robustness of the school's data on their students, because "our kind of students move a lot, their phones get disconnected, they get new phones. Just *finding* them is a big deal." Aaron described the doorknockers as a type of charming census taker, motivated mostly by concerns for the student's well-being and the quality of the school's data.

But when I asked, Aaron conceded that the doorknockers are also part of the school's institutional plan to reduce student loan defaults and dropout rates. When students complete their paperwork for federal student loans, the application asks for references. Student loan servicers use those references in their debt-collection practices if the student is late or defaults on the student loan. The doorknockers were the school's way of giving student loan servicers better data on references, but they were also a way to head off defaults at the pass by keeping close tabs on where students could be found. That kind of individual-level data on where students live, how often they move, and under what circumstances they move could tell us a lot about the context within which students at for-profit colleges make their educational choices. Additionally, the context of those choices could help us to suss out whether poor for-profit college dropouts and graduates are poor because of the conditions they bring with them to school, what happens to them in school, and—potentially most powerful—what does *not* happen for them when they go (back) to school.

Aaron says that this is exactly one of the ways the school where he works that data: "We hired a marketing firm once to give us profiles on who our likely students are, just to get a check on what we had gleaned from all this data we collect. We have massive amounts of this stuff. Anyway, the marketing firm told us that we were pretty dead-to-rights on our understanding of our market. But they also laughed and said they'd never seen such cleanly segmented market data before. Our student profiles are precise, and they work." How were those profiles so powerful, I asked? "Well, for instance, we brought in a Freudian psychoanalyst once to do what they do with our students. She found that our students—almost all of them are women, by the way—were stuck in a moment of trauma from their lives." Could he say more? "They have had some truly horrible things happen to them, Tressie . . ." Aaron trails off for a moment, genuinely, it seems, touched by the stories his data had revealed about their students. "When they come to us, most of these women have been beaten or abused or . . ."

"Raped," I provide.

"Yes."

"And this matters to how you enroll students?"

"Absolutely. The analyst said our students were looking for and would respond to what she called 'the good-enough mother.' That's a caring authority figure who isn't perfect but who could help them move past the trauma where many of them are still fixed and frozen; for many of them this is infantilizing. They're adult women still behaving the age they were when they were traumatized!"

These behaviors spilled over into the classroom. "Our students, they fight. I mean, we have some campuses that are 100 percent female. They come from the same neighborhoods and they fight over men or all kinds of things." These behaviors, born of the kind of trauma that is often associated with poverty, also make it hard for students to get a job. "Our business advisory board tells us that our students don't always know how to behave at work. And when we follow up with the employers where our students got a call back and an interview, they say it's the behavior stuff that was a problem." That's descriptive, but what about this changes how the school is organized? "We took the good-enough mother idea and hired a lot of women in the key college roles. A lot of our campus directors, the enrollment advisers, they're women. Our kind of student responds to them."

Aaron had pulled back the curtain on something I had noticed in my research and something I had experienced while working in for-profit colleges. At the nine schools where I had conducted re-search, seven of the nine enrollment counselors were women. And when I visited the campuses, the staff was predominately female in all nine cases. From the receptionist that greeted me to those in academic and support roles, women were conspicuously present, just as men were conspicuously dominant in jobs like Aaron's, the leadership and operations side of the colleges. All of the admissions and staff at the Beauty College were women, save one male instructor. But that was cosmetology, a female-dominated profession. Aaron's school focused on business and healthcare, but had the same employee dynamics. That suggested it was less about the particular field of training and more about research-driven hiring choices that would best mesh with the needs of a school's "kind of students."

Other for-profit college executives told me similar stories, although none quite as detailed as Aaron's. A senior operations officer of a for-profit college that primarily enrolls enlisted military and their spouses told me that the best thing about that student body was that the school didn't have to motivate them. "If I have a problem with a soldier, I tell him I'm going to call his CO (commanding officer)," he said. The enrollment staff at this college competed for the assignment because the paperwork was streamlined, there were no nosy parents, and they did not have to work to find or track their students. When Uncle Sam owns you, your school doesn't need door-knockers.

The academic director of another for-profit college described how the enrollment process at her school pushed their students to risk going to college. "They need to believe they can do it," she told me. This school had a sizable interest in graduate degrees. The academic director did not deal directly with enrollment unless a student was delinquent or was in danger of losing financial aid eligibility for an academic reason. From her perspective, the enrollment process provided "tough love" that many of "these people" needed.

After reading some of my work and reflecting on his experiences, Aaron was clearly conflicted about whether or not he was helping students he now knew were unprivileged in ways that ran far deeper than their being underserved by traditional higher education. He wanted to brainstorm ways to make the system better. "What our students really need is childcare, Tressie," he said. "I've imagined it. Why aren't there childcare centers and public resource offices next door to each of our schools?! We'd make a killing if they were and, yes, make their lives better, too. That's a win-win." I explained that this was a well-understood problem. Community colleges, historically black colleges, and public colleges—the kinds of schools that have long served non-traditional and unprivileged students—have tried to do exactly what Aaron was describing. I gently pointed out that childcare centers are even more regulated and potentially litigious than are college campuses.

Many schools, faced with severe declines in their financial support, have moved away from the expense and risk of offering childcare. The National Coalition for Campus Children's Centers at the University of Wisconsin–Madison says that "community colleges with on-campus childcare centers declined from 53 percent in 2003–04 to 46 percent in 2013."[36] These are institutions that we think of as being most friendly or most suitable for students like those Aaron tracked. The tuition is cheaper and the services more plentiful. But without childcare or limited childcare options, someone like London might find it more feasible to finish a certificate quickly at Aaron's for-profit college than to risk a cheaper option at the community college. The traditional degree-granting colleges also saw a decline in campus childcare: public 4-year institutions declined from 54 percent to 52 percent from 2002 to 2013. Aaron did not know it but his ideas had been commonplace in public higher education and had only declined as his for-profit was ascending. And community colleges are always innovating ways to bring "wrap-around services," the kind like the resource centers Aaron imagined, into the college milieu to better serve students who need them. Single Stop USA programs are a current version of this. These programs literally aim to be a single stop for financial and social resources for students.

Aaron had, on his own, come to some of the most complicated and well-researched areas in the sociology of education. How can a college remediate the interlocking, systemic, entrenched, and inheritable conditions of poverty, near-poverty, and inequality? However, the realities of the school where Aaron worked made his question more complicated than it appeared. How can a college *that is honor-bound to extract excess tuition* remediate the interlocking, systemic, entrenched, and inheritable conditions of poverty, near-poverty, and inequality? Everything Aaron suggested not only existed but also cost a lot of money and resources. I told him as much, and he smiled wistfully. With a little sigh, he said, "Well, our business clients (the private-sector actors the school maintains relationships with to vet their curriculum and ideally to hire their graduates) have already told us that they love our students' job readiness. But they want them to be more ready, faster, and cheaper to hire." By cheaper, the employers meant willing and able to work for less wages while being skilled enough to do ever more complex tasks. "They've moved beyond simple training in medical billing and what have you. Now our students need to know how to interpret records information and make decisions based on it," he said. "We can do that. We can train them to do that. But it takes time."

More time takes more money, and for the students borrowing to be in school it means taking on more student loans and eventually having a higher debt burden to repay. Aaron realized the conundrum. He was proud of his school's mission. He was proud of the faculty and staff, the good-enough mothers who were "incredibly committed" to the students. He was very proud of the students who lived with their trauma and still came to school. He was proud of the sophisticated research the school does. But he was a numbers guy trained in some of the best numbers programs in the country. He knew the numbers didn't add up. To make cheaper workers faster, he would have to either enroll vastly different students or eat up the profit margin of a school that was, above all, a business.

4

WHEN HIGHER EDUCATION
MAKES CENTS

In 2015, I spoke with Janet, a middle-class woman in her mid-thirties who was enrolled in an on-campus doctoral program and who, despite carrying a six-figure federal student debt load, was looking into her private loan options. I asked Janet why she continued at the for-profit school she was attending knowing the cost was more than she could afford to pay. Janet looked at me in a way that could only be described as her thinking I was completely crazy. "Education is an *investment*," she said.

In the first three chapters, I argued that the best way to understand the expansion of for-profit colleges is through inequalities and changes in work. The latter makes going to college the only practical choice for obtaining a good job. The former constrains where a person can go to college and determines not only one's risk to pay for it but also how well that risk pays off. Now, it's time for a closer look at how decisions that some of us find perplexing seem quite sensible to no small number of people who are looking to survive and thrive in the new economy. From "call now" to enrollment to maxing out on federal aid, this chapter will explore the thinking, rationales, and processes at play when people—including smart, savvy students like Janet—decide to attend a for-profit college.

I've made the case that the root cause of the Wall Street era of for-profit colleges was a broader ideological shift instead of a rational consequence of demand or inevitable outcome of deregulation.

William Tierney, former president of the nation's largest academic association of education researchers, places for-profits' contemporary genesis at the intersection of declining public subsidies and increased consumer demand. Economist Richard Vedder identifies a similar starting point, but Vedder also makes a finer point on the elitism of traditional higher education as conditioning unmet consumer demand. Attorney David Halperin has been a staunch public critic and researcher of for-profit higher education. His point of entry tends to be the federal student aid system and deregulation of higher education. These are all true. They are the social and political conditions that were present at the start of for-profit colleges' rapid expansion. However, even taken together, they do not provide the whole story.

Critics of neoliberalism fairly point out that in the new economy, corporate responsibility continues to shift exposure to risk onto workers and families. As other capital markets dry up, the interests held in the public trust become drinking holes in the desert to the investment class. But neoliberalism predates the start of the Wall Street era of higher education. More specifically, the rise of the finance class as an elite interest group with a cohesive ideology—what many simply dub "financialization"—not only made this transformation right but also ordered how it would take place: shareholder organizations, subsidiaries, and capital investment. Social scientists have pegged financialization to the decline of union power, since financialization is mostly unchecked by a labor voice. It is instructive to note that faculty at for-profit colleges are not unionized, as are most faculty in traditional higher education.[1] Indeed, in marketing and financial-advisement documents, the lack of unionization is frequently touted as evidence that the sector is a viable investment.

Unchecked financialization and challenges to labor rights have happened across every sector of social life, and the political choices and dynamics previously discussed have aided and abetted the expansion of risky education credentials. Simultaneously, these same conditions produced the pulling apart of "good" and "bad" labor markets, and such job polarization produced a set of competitive pressures at the top and in the middle. Economists, education researchers, and marketers are blithely calling these competitive pressures "consumer demand," an essentially neutered designation. This label strips these processes of their political conditions, making them seem like natural and unavoidable choices made by individuals. The fallacy that the swift rise of for-profit colleges is simply the result of consumer demand—as if demand isn't shaped by the aforementioned forces—makes critiquing the privatization of higher education seem unnatural. This framing poisons the well from which good social inquiry emerges, making polemics of policy and turning empirical research into prescription and culture wars.

That is the big picture, but as promised I'll paint a smaller one to reveal the detail. The appeal of for-profit education to financiers is clear. At the most superficial level, it is also apparent how so-called flexible degree programs might appeal to workers who cannot afford the opportunity costs of exiting the labor market in order to get the credentials they need to stay competitive. Still, for-profit colleges wind up appealing to a wide range of potential students. These prospects are often compared to those in community colleges because most of the current for-profit credentials have historically been sub-baccalaureate degrees and certificates, similar to those that community colleges confer. Yet, the fastest growing subsector of for-profit colleges isn't in lower-level degrees but in bachelor's, graduate, and professional degrees. How, then, do for-profit colleges manage to appeal successfully to GED holders and traditionally educated master's students alike? Their model of recruitment and enrollment maximizes something similarly valuable across diverse groups: time. Time has become the commodity being traded for institutional prestige.

Let's All Admit—There's Time to Enroll

Aaron, the marketing executive from Chapter 3, gave me an idea of how nuanced student data collected by for-profit corporations shapes various parts of the for-profit college apparatus. Who is most likely to call a for-profit college is steeped in various structural inequalities, a fact that made me wonder in what other ways their organizational structure tapped into those inequalities. I knew from my time spent on the inside that few stages of the process are as vital to the for-profit college mission as enrolling new students. It is arguably the single most critical part of the process for these schools to get right. It is expensive, which is why for-profit colleges devote more of their operating budgets to advertising and recruitment than they do to instruction and counseling. To understand what kinds of students a credentialing organization is designed for, one can study for whom the organization's most critical functions work best.

I had my experience in for-profit colleges, and by 2011 things had changed since my time working in them. The new economy that was really just beginning to take hold in the early 2000s was now considered by many to be the dominant mode of work for the typical U.S. worker. That also happened to be the period in which shareholder for-profit colleges found a very receptive investment and regulatory audience. And it was the period during which for-profit colleges had moved beyond the "typical" likely student to increasingly enroll more affluent students in higher-level degree programs. What these dissimilar groups have in common that the for-profit college process so efficiently zeroes in on—to the tune of billions of dollars in tuition revenue—is a lack of time. Whether there was barely any extra time in their days, little extra time in their work week, or no time to waste before earning a better wage to make ends meet, they all possessed a real and present sense of urgency.

In 2012 and 2013, I enrolled in nine for-profit colleges in a city where there is no shortage of higher education options. According to one city document, Atlanta, Georgia, has one of the densest clusters of higher education institutions in the country. It also has one of the most robust systems of public, community, and historically black colleges. These colleges are arguably known for enrolling the kinds of students that are increasingly enrolling in for-profit colleges. If you go to a for-profit college in Atlanta, Georgia, it is not for want of traditional college options. I called or contacted each of the nine institutions (a mix chosen to represent the sector's diversity) as any prospective student would. And then I leaned out of the process, letting the enrollment counselors and organizational steps guide me rather than actively trying to shape the processes to suit my needs and tastes. The point was to behave as similar to the likely prospective student as possible. I could not change who or what I was—namely, a middle-class, African American doctoral student. But I could choose not to act on who I was, which would effectively throw up roadblocks in a process that had presumably not been designed for the likes of me.

The enrollment process is most remarkable for how rapid it is and for what it does *not* assume about prospective students. While I was going around town enrolling in for-profit colleges, first I hoped to sort out whether an intensive revenue-generating enrollment process happens at for-profit colleges *because* they operate for profit. If the experience of enrolling were different at different kinds of for-profit colleges, I could then ascertain that this is not the case. As you'll see, the process was nearly uniform at nine campuses, each offering different levels and types of degrees. Once I gleaned that the enrollment path was specifically linked to the colleges' for-profit designation, I became interested in finding out the types of things they assume (about their likely students) that speak to and draw in the Mikes and Londons of the world.

———

Perhaps nothing about the for-profit college enrollment process is more distinct than how fast it is. Studying this phenomenon, Tierney and Guilbert C. Hentschke note that "students generally are admitted the day they apply or make their enrollment deposit." I found this to be true as I enrolled in nine distinct for-profit colleges. The customer service ethos that researchers commonly associate with for-profit schools is thought to maximize a prospective student's most precious commodity—time. The typical time from the first point of contact to the first possible day I could start class was a little more than eighteen days. At five different schools, an enrollment counselor said that if I showed up for the rest of my appointments like I had for the campus tour, there was no reason that I could not start courses at the next available start date. The process is also fast because there are few bureaucratic hand-off points as students negotiate various institutional offices. At each of the nine colleges, I had a single point of contact: the enrollment officer (EO). In six cases, the EO was the same person with whom I spoke during the first contact on the telephone. The only other suggested interaction was with a financial aid counselor with whom I would meet after completing the enrollment paperwork.

Enrolling in a for-profit college requires just two steps. First, a student must make first contact with the institution. This could be making a phone call, completing an online information form, or responding to an online solicitation. After the first contact is made, the first interaction between the EO and the student is a telephone conversation. The EO guides the conversation using mostly closed-ended questions, similar to selling techniques that manufacture consent. The aim of the EO is to gain consent from the student to take a tour of the campus. Once a campus tour is scheduled, the second step of the process commences. The campus tour includes an informational interview wherein the EO gathers additional contact information for the student, and often for family and friends, and prompts the prospect for vignettes that describe their career aspirations.

There is an information sheet to complete at each school, none longer than two pages. It includes contact information and four to six questions about aspirations, work experience, and interests. This is the only document introduced throughout the whole process that is comparable to a traditional college application. Next, the EO guides the student through the campus facility and highlights features that will help the student attain their career goals. Once the tour concludes, the student is led back to an interview room for a discussion on the specifics of the next available start date, degree programs available, and tuition. Then the EO presents an enrollment agreement. The agreement is similar to the terms and conditions riders common to purchasing a car or a time-share property. All of the enrollment agreements require an enrollment fee of approximately forty-five dollars. The fee could be paid by cash, check, or credit card. At two of the colleges I toured, I was offered an installment plan with an initial payment as low as five dollars.

Call Now: The Telephone Interview

When a prospective student responds to a marketing exhortation to "call now to start your new career," he is greeted not by an automated phone prompt but a person, even when a phone call is made as late as 9 p.m. My online requests received telephone responses as early as 8:15 a.m. the following business day (Monday through Saturday, in most cases). An EO conducts the call, as opposed to a receptionist or administrative assistant. In seven of the nine calls I made, the enrollment officer was a woman. She guided the content and pacing of the conversation. She gathered contact information "in case we are disconnected." Next, there were two to three questions about "what made you decide to change your life

today?" They asked about my career aspirations, current work arrangements, and social support networks: "What does your family think about your returning to school?"

The phone interviews lasted fourteen minutes, on average. In
each case, the EO said that the best way to have my questions answered or to "get a feel for where [I] will be going to school" would
be to schedule a campus tour as soon as possible. I was not presented with appointment times or business hours. Instead, the enrollment officer ascertained my schedule availability and offered
me one or two possible times. The choices were always within a
seventy-two-hour window. They always resisted setting a time
more than a week in advance. Token resistance—for example, saying that I did not have transportation—was countered by offers to
meet evenings and weekends or to bring a friend (who could drive
me) along for the tour. Questions and assumptions about my family structure and parental status figured prominently in the telephone interviews. The following exchange with an EO accurately
illustrates the style and tone I encountered at every school. The
process simultaneously establishes rapport and captures critical
information needed to enroll me:

> And you can bring your children for the tour. They should see
> where their mom is going to school! [I responded that I do not
> have any children.] Oh, that's great! Good for you. Get your life
> together before you have a family. That's the best way to go. So,
> can you come tomorrow at 6:15 p.m.?

Once a campus tour was scheduled, the EO called to remind
me of the appointment. If the appointment was more than two
days out (which was the case for five of the nine visits I made),
the enrollment counselor called twice: once the day before and
again on the day of the appointment. Enrollment officers remembered my name and usually pronounced it correctly; often, they

also referenced some personal or specific detail, such as what route I would be taking from my job.

Visit Today, Classes Starting Soon: The Campus Tour

Like almost all applicants to for-profit colleges, when I arrived for the campus tour I was greeted by a receptionist, told that my EO was expecting me, and given an information sheet to complete while I waited. The sheet, typically one or two pages long, asked for all forms of contact information and had some combination of short-answer questions that largely focused on my motivations, anticipated roadblocks to college success, and referrals of other prospective students.

Once the sheet was complete, or ten minutes had elapsed (often the latter happened before the former and the EO waived completing the form), the EO greeted me. The EO was generally warm and upbeat, authoritative but not intimidating. She took the information sheet, and it stayed with her for the remainder of the campus tour. She led us both to some sort of semi-private room, generally small but well appointed. The spaces varied in size and poshness, but in each case there were doors, and they were closed once the interview began. We generally started with a brief discussion akin to professional small talk. We talked about the traffic into the campus, if it was conveniently located, or if I got lost. If I had, the representative offered a better route. In most cases, she mentioned a detail from our phone conversation. "Now, you said you're on the east side of town right? Did you come down (highway) 20 or come through town?"

There was often a congratulatory moment wherein the EO validated my decision as important. "You're making the first step to getting your degree! Good for you," one middle-aged woman told me during this phase of introductory small talk. The congratulations not only validated my decision to "invest in myself" but it also moved the discussion into matters more directly relevant to enrolling.

The casual conversation then pivoted to being directed by information on the sheet I had completed when I arrived, now in the enrollment officer's constant possession. What happened next varied somewhat from school to school. At six of them, the EO launched directly into a presentation about what that particular for-profit institution offered or further probed me for potential obstacles to "achieving my dream." That probing usually centered on whether my parents or significant other supported my educational plans, or the details of my work schedule. Three of the enrollment officers skipped directly to a tour of the facilities. In every conversation, I signaled that I did not have a partner and that I worked most weekdays until 6 p.m. There was often visible relief when I mentioned having no romantic partners. One EO commented on my good decision to "focus on [myself]" at this important juncture of my life. Once it had been determined that there was a program or schedule that would address any obstacles I had presented, we moved into a general discussion of the school's offerings.

The program portion of the appointment was analogous to the brochures found at and mailed by the recruitment offices at traditional universities. Like those shiny brochures with smiling, diverse student faces, the campus tours were positive in tone and thin on specifics. For example, one technology school told me about the growing field of technology, that their professors were former practitioners, and that the school offered sixteen different programs. Also like a brochure, there were no details on tuition, coursework requirements, or how long it would take to earn any of the degrees. By this point in our meeting, at most of the schools (seven of the nine), we had yet to discuss my specific program of interest. Five of the information sheets asked about my broad career goals, but only one asked specifically what program I intended to enroll in at that institution. At the other institutions, it wasn't until after we had established the convenience of my commute, my good decision-making skills, and the value of a degree in fast-growing fields that we discussed specific programs. I was presented with two, never more than three, programs that were offered at the times I had indicated I would be available. I was not asked to commit to any of the choices, but rather whether "any of these appeal to [me]." A general signal of agreement then moved us on to a tour of the facilities.

The facilities tour was generally brief, perhaps designed to limit the time commitment required by prospective students, but in addition there was rarely a lot of square footage to cover. All but one site was in an office park. The "campus" was usually several floors of an office building or a stand-alone building entirely occupied by the college. The tour included a visit to some kind of social space, be it a canteen with vending machines or a well-appointed conference-sized room with seats and a television. It also boasted a visit to a job board, a classroom, and a "resource" room.

At almost every stop during the tour, the enrollment officer linked aspects of the facility to a need she had inferred from our phone and interview conversations. I was particularly struck by how the EO used questioning techniques that made it difficult to answer any way but affirmatively. For example, at one allied health college, the EO asked, "So, do you think this lounge would help you get in a snack when you're running late?" On eleven separate occasions at nine schools, the EO said of a job board, "You mentioned that you're looking for a more professional job. Do you think this career board might help you keep an eye out for a better job?" These types of questions were phrased so that a negative response would be either a non sequitur—"No, I don't think a microwave, fridge, and vending machine with sandwiches would help me to snack"—or would violate a social norm, like admitting that you didn't really want to keep an eye out for a better job. The tour concluded by returning to the front office or to a private room. Until this point, no specific details had been divulged about the cost of tuition, the program or major that I might choose, or the next available start dates for my chosen path. Seated and comfortable again, these details were now offered by the EO along with a friendly command to "enroll today" by signing a multi-page enrollment agreement akin to the terms and conditions of an automobile purchase. Think endless small print that no one in their right mind would sit and read on the spot.

Enrollment and Admissions at Traditional and For-Profit Colleges

Enrolling in a variety of for-profit colleges revealed the breadth, depth, and diversity of the enrollment process that I had worked in well before I had any concept of the many forces and structures influencing it. The exercise also shows how students can be demographically different yet have similar needs, but for different reasons. For poorer or lower-status students, the enrollment process works because it spackles over the gaps in cultural capital needed to navigate the traditional college admissions process. For higher-status students, the same enrollment process works because of what Arlie Hochschild coined "the time bind," a conundrum that impacts all but the wealthiest. The time bind refers to the blurring of the lines between home and work, when the latter never really ends. As competition for work increases, the blurring intensifies and makes "flexibility" more than a choice; it becomes imperative in order to manage multiple competitive pressures.

The commonalities of the for-profit college enrollment process are not embedded in the connections between institutions. They are rooted in the shared social conditions of groups that do not have those institutional connections. They are not drawing from secondary schools, formal or informal college preparatory programs, civic or social groups. Essentially, for-profit colleges are not drawing from institutional connections that are different from those tapped by traditional universities. They operate in response to the reality that millions of prospective students exist outside the social machinery that delivers people to college. Elite students are generally born with connections to institutions, including boarding schools, social clubs, and peer groups—arrangements that provide links and implicit knowledge that admissions officers at elite colleges reward. Campus visitors to elite universities have described a "kinship among people in the waiting room." [2] Their children had attended the same high schools, they summered together, and they had run into each other on unrequired, informal college tours at similarly prestigious campuses. These "typical students" were the preferred fuel for the "college's organizational machinery." [3]

Less-selective institutions also have typical students. These two- and four-year schools tend to have few admissions requirements. Most have histories as land-grant colleges and junior colleges with "open door" missions. However, it isn't as clear that the typical students at less-selective institutions are the organizational machinery's preferred fuel. Like for-profit colleges, community colleges in particular "serve as the point of entry for students who wouldn't otherwise participate in postsecondary education." [4] The "point of entry" does not extend to the actual process of gaining admission at a less-selective college. An online survey of every branch of a community college in Atlanta found that all of them encouraged students to enroll online. One of the city's largest community colleges boasted a graphic flowchart for admissions. The first three steps were to "let us get to know you" by 1) completing an online contact form; 2) submitting an online application at an external state university website; and 3) acquiring an institutional identification number and uploading your documents. Listed after the three steps were four additional steps: 1) submit final documents; 2) verify tuition classification; 3) set an institutional email password; and 4) complete orientation. There is an additional sidebar reminding students to complete their federal financial aid forms

by following the directions available at the institution's financial
aid webpage.

It took nine clicks to find detailed information about speaking
with an admissions counselor. It also required a fair amount of
institutional translation. For example, the admissions page with
the two sets of multiple application steps is called Admissions. But
the eventual name and webpage for the office that administers admissions assistance is called Advising. Additionally, advising for
first-time students is only conducted "at New Student Orientation
with a faculty member." The financial aid office is open Monday,
Tuesday, Thursday, and Friday from 8 a.m. to 5 p.m. with extended hours through 7 p.m. on Wednesday. The advising office's
hours are similar, with its extended day held on Tuesday. The college had three application deadlines and three fixed new-student
class start times.

The admissions process at both elite and non-elite institutions is
most efficient when prospective students have middle-class social
resources.[5] Middle-class children, no matter their race, are social-
ized to assume that bureaucratic systems should respond to their
needs. Their parents give them the language skills, confidence, and
support to engage their teachers as equals. As my experience navigating the website of an open-admissions college can attest, verbal
and written skills are grist for the bureaucratic mill (e.g., completing online forms, sending emails). When students cut from this
cloth manage to negotiate competing deadlines, personalities, and
norms among the multiple offices they must navigate to complete
the traditional college admissions process, they are rewarded with
fewer obstacles. The bureaucracy responds favorably to the social
resources that cultivated those skills in the first place.

In contrast, the enrollment process I experienced at for-profit
institutions never once assumed that I had been cultivated to navigate a complex bureaucracy. Neither was it assumed that I should
develop such acuity. The phone call was short, about fourteen
minutes. Unless I presented an objection to scheduling a campus

tour, the enrollment officers guided the direction of the telephone conversation. The same was true of the campus tour. I had only to answer the enrollment officers' questions to move through the process successfully. Additionally, the information sheets I filled out upon my arrival were brief, requiring little writing. Perhaps most interesting is that an organizational form predicated on its technological innovation did not require an online application to initiate or complete the enrollment process.

I need never even revisit a bureaucracy with which I presumably had experience: my high school. The enrollment officers would navigate ordering my transcripts for me. Indeed, the enrollment process was noticeably halted only when I attempted to control its trajectory. At one appointment, I mildly insisted on knowing the price of tuition at the start of the campus tour. I mentioned that price was important to me. The enrollment officer said that I was "smart to keep an eye on my budget" but declined to give me the price. She took the opportunity to reiterate that the for-profit institution she represented offered aid and grants and that she would "break that all down" for me later. When I asked again, more directly, the enrollment officer slid a sheet with the tuition amount into a folder and gave it to me. She was noticeably upset about the disruption. She relaxed once I thanked her and placed the folder in my bag without opening it.

Traditional colleges benefit from a deeply entrenched cultural faith in the value of college, particularly among higher-status groups.[6] Selective colleges can readily assume that their prospective students' journeys to the admissions office began long ago as they internalized parental and social expectations.[7] Therefore, traditional colleges invest little time or money in convincing prospective students that college is a valuable proposition. For-profit colleges, on the other hand, assume that their likely student has a different process for assessing the value of college.[8] They are not organized to leverage a default assumption about the intrinsic value of college. Instead, they are organized to leverage the ephemeral moment when a prospective student's perception of her changing economic or social fortunes prompts her to consider going to college.

I gathered a few of the shiny brochures about my own campus, where I was working on a graduate degree, to compare with the spiel and the materials I was given when I took the campus tours. The materials from my school all took great care to market how their college is not just college, but a singular collegiate experience. In contrast, on almost all of the campus tours I was presented first and foremost with generic value statements about higher education. One enrollment officer said that "nothing pays like a degree" because "these days everybody's got one." Another said that I would "make a million dollars more over my lifetime" with a college degree than with a high school diploma. Time and again, enrollment officers sold me on the value proposition of higher education before they told me anything specific about their college.

Traditional universities can assume that their likely student understands the value of higher education, because most middle-class and wealthy students do. Of the Ivy League students she studied, sociologist Anne Mullen says that they were an articulate, reflective group that could wax poetic about their life's goals until she asked them to describe how they had decided to go to college. The Yale students did not understand the question, because they had, of course, "always been going to college." When pushed, the students said they guess their parents had expected college for them, but they could not separate their parents' expectations from their own aspirations.[9]

As I noted, EOs established frequent telephone contact during both parts of the prospective-student enrollment process. After I completed each campus tour without paying the enrollment fee that would finalize my enrollment, the EO called me regularly for weeks. Most of these calls were friendly in tone but insistent. They reminded me of how I wanted to "get off the merry-go-round and get ahead." One enrollment officer used my mother's name in a message that urged me to "make [her] proud." They reminded me that I had done the right thing, made the right choice, and they wanted to help me succeed.

Training documents obtained by a Senate investigation into the for-profit college sector call this process the "pain funnel." [10] It is designed to "poke the pain points" of wavering prospective students to remind them of why they need a degree. Ethical considerations aside, the pain funnel is not entirely unlike how "helicopter parents" are described: pushy, aggressive, and desiring the best for their student-child.[11] Indeed, one ad for a for-profit college says of their enrollment officers that "if you miss a class, [EO] calls. Need an ear? She'll listen. Fall behind? She'll help. She's like your mom . . . without all the guilt."

Gendered parent roles in middle-class groups have been held forth as an example of competitive mobility gone amok. The "tiger mom" caricature has joined many others in media accounts of pushy families that won't let their children leave the nest.[12] Beyond stereotypes and anecdotes, assumptions about family resources and support are the most deeply embedded in the path through traditional higher education. College applications ask for details about an applicant's parents. College tours and open houses generally assume parents will attend to ask the important questions and fan the flames of motivation throughout a student's matriculation.

The bottom line is that educational attainment in a bureaucratic structure requires motivation, whether that motivation is created by a system's structure of opportunity, family pressure or values, legal legitimacy, or through a university's admissions practices. Some students find themselves aspiring to a college education without the usual corresponding behaviors that traditional college admissions assume successful applicants will have. Should economic or social change incentivize enrolling in college, what will motivate these students to negotiate the strange, time-consuming process of decoding prestige hierarchies, admissions guidelines, and multiple deadlines? The enrollment process at for-profit colleges assumes little to no sustained individual motivation from students to complete the process. Beyond the first call and showing up when prodded, the motivation is all in the structure.

Sociologist Mitchell Stevens describes a guidance counselor at an elite high school he visited during his ethnography of elite college admissions as "a beloved nanny assigned the task of ushering her charges into college."[13] There is a vast educational industrial complex of counselors, guidebooks, and privileged information that can be bought for the right price.[14] In truth, some of them are not just "like" a nanny aiming to get well-heeled students into the right college; they are full-on, full-service college app nannies. There are even private college admissions consultants for hire who provide services that range from targeting safety schools to writing college essays and orchestrating meetings with key decision makers at the nation's most competitive colleges. In contrast to students with access to the formal organizational mechanisms that deliver them from better-funded public and private schools to the best colleges, non-elite students must navigate a largely implicit admissions process without the vast store of social resources which the system is designed to reward. Should they somehow manage to navigate the formal processes, the informal ones remain largely opaque and inaccessible. It takes social capital to know about services like admissions consultants, and financial capital to pay for them once you're hip to the game. Which brings us back to the issue that vexes both highly educated researchers and the people who talk to me on the bus. Why do students pay so much to go to a for-profit college? The mounds of data I have collected provide some clues.

Price is absolute. If the tuition is $37,000, then the price is $37,000. Cost, on the other hand, is relative. It is relative not only to the means one has to pay the price, but also to one's position in the social structure and in the labor market. In a small case study at a for-profit college, education researchers Constance Iloh and William Tierney found that students viewed price as an indicator of value, not as an indicator of low prestige. Still, they could not fully explain the complexities of why (and how) that is the case or why it would work across groups with vastly different knowledge bases. To address those complexities, I took up David K. Brown and David B. Bills's call for sociologists to examine these credentialing complexities using ethnographic tools and an eye on how and why institutions become stratified by prestige. What resulted was a close examination of students enrolled in for-profit colleges, one that offers a different and deeper understanding of how students make sense of their for-profit college choices.

Men Lie, Women Lie, Numbers Don't Lie

I didn't find the online group Sisters Working to Achieve Greatness (SWAG)—it found me. Someone knew that I was black, a woman, and in a PhD program. That was enough to be invited to join SWAG, a community that stayed connected mostly online. As it happened, almost all of the members—"Swaggers," they called themselves—were enrolled in online PhD programs at one of the three largest for-profit colleges: the University of Phoenix, Capella University, and Walden University. After lurking for a few months, I asked the group moderator what she knew about the members. She volunteered a survey of SWAG members. Two-thirds of the 1,719 group members had completed the survey. The survey collected demographic, degree, and institutional information. This gave me a good sense of who was in the group, data that were confirmed as I spent two to three hours each week participating in the group over the course of nine months in 2014. I identified myself as a researcher doing a research project on nontraditional schools. (I used that language bearing in mind the Public Agenda and Kresge Foundation study that suggested the phrase "for-profit college" rarely resonates with the students who attend them.)

I asked the moderator for permission to recruit interview participants for my project.[15] I shared my research protocols documentation approving the research. I reposted my name, contact information, and affiliations regularly to the group so that the information stayed fairly close to the top of the discussion board. Over six months, I interviewed twenty-nine Swaggers. I asked them about their educational biographies, how they understood their degrees, and how they imagined their future work and family lives. I also obtained their permission to reference, in my writing and analysis, posts they had made to the group. Together, we revisited some of those posts so that I could ask clarifying questions or spark their memory of an event. Swaggers taught me important things about for-profit colleges and the students who are enrolled to earn so-called upmarket degrees. First, they taught me how they perceived the value of their degree, a degree that many disdain without knowing much more than a school's tagline. They also taught me that when we assume that they make educational choices based on prestige and cost, we miss the true context of their decisions. Finally, they taught me how we are all complicit in reinforcing the distinctions between Lower Ed and Higher Ed.

Swaggers were pursuing degrees across six disciplines: education, organizational science, business, clinical psychology, nursing, and communications. A doctoral degree is an expensive undertaking for African American, Hispanic, working-class, and first-generation students in almost any institutional context.[16] Students who do not benefit from the largesse of generational wealth and a privileged status are more likely to incur debt in graduate school, even when their programs provide modest stipends and tuition scholarships. However, it remains true that for-profit colleges have fewer alternatives by which Swaggers can avoid debt. For-profit online degree programs cannot offer graduate and teaching assistantships or institutional aid, so earning a PhD in them is especially expensive. Of the posts that offered a number, students reported borrowing from $92,000 to $180,000 for all of their degrees, up to and including their doctoral debt. Like most students in for-profit colleges, Swaggers reported paying for their degrees through federal student loan programs. Generally the "free" grant money—funds that do not need to be repaid—does not apply to graduate study. These women were primarily using student loans that must be paid back after they graduate or withdraw from school. Paying for their PhDs was a significant concern for many Swaggers, thus posts about debt were not in short supply.

Debt. This is where people think for-profit students should hear a loud warning bell, especially when their tuition debt piles up and they come close to "maxing out." Students max out when they exceed the borrowing limits on federal loans. Currently, graduate and professional school students may borrow up to $20,500 per year from the unsubsidized Federal Stafford loan program. The cumulative loan limits are $138,500, including undergraduate debt. If someone is maxing out, that means she has over $130,000 in student loan debt. Why would a student take on so much debt for a graduate degree from a for-profit college? The ideology around higher education costs sheds some light on this topic.

By the 1980s, the idea of college as a public trust was shifting—swept up in a wave of disinvestment in all things public. The ethos changed, and people in all corners began to think of college as an individual investment. This shift away from understanding higher education as something that was important and good for society as a whole made the politics of financializing college tuition a sensible public choice. This attitude and the attendant policy changes proliferated: declining state investments in public higher education, austerity policies at community colleges and four-year colleges, incentives for universities to act more "entrepreneurial" and raise money. In effect, we told students that higher education was a private good with social rewards. Based on this, students should invest even as colleges increasingly shifted the cost of attendance to students. Investment implies risks and rewards. And for many of the students I speak to in for-profit colleges, investment also implies size and scope.

Janet was thirty-five years old, and this was her third time in college. She had attended a private historically black college and a night school program, and at the time that we spoke she was enrolled in an on-campus, for-profit doctoral degree program. We communicated online for months before we officially sat down to talk. When we did, I started by asking her to fill in some of the gaps of those online conversations. In particular, I was interested in how Janet made sense of her financial difficulties at her for-profit college. "I could not afford to sit in [be enrolled] one semester," she said. Janet had written about maxing out on her student loans. How did that work? "[My university financial aid counselor] told me that I didn't have enough [student aid eligibility] left for the next year. I got that email!" The email she was referring to is what others like Janet, enrolled in for-profit graduate degree programs, called the notification sent out to students who were reaching their maximum loan eligibility. "Getting that email" was talked about in a joking way, the way we often make jokes of personal troubles to turn them into public foibles.

Janet had posted a "bat signal" to Swaggers looking for leads on getting the funding she needed to complete her degree. "I had come to [sic] far to give up now," she wrote, adopting a line from a classic black gospel song. Friends, online and off, directed her to a private student loan company, but Janet knew that her "credit was probably too bad to get one. They use credit." Unlike federal student loans, private student loans use standard credit scoring criteria in their lending.[17] They also charge more in fees and in interest and do not have the same options for payment forgiveness should debtors have problems repaying. By all accounts, private student loans are riskier and a real albatross around the neck of for-profit college students who, in particular, rely on them because their tuition is higher.

As I shared in the opening of this chapter, I asked Janet why she kept forging ahead when it was quite clear that she could not afford to pay the cost. She insisted that education is an investment. The language of investment came up often among all the for-profit students I talked to. It came up most often among the most upwardly mobile, higher-status students like Janet and Mike. Some had traditional college backgrounds. All but two of them were enrolled in graduate or professional degree programs. All of them had taken on debt they considered significant. For many of us, the high debt loads among for-profit college students are the single biggest cause for alarm—and for judgment. We assume that students like Janet would or should be similarly alarmed. That is because we're thinking about the cost as *debt*. When thought of as an investment, high tuition makes perfectly good sense. What are the rules of investing? We tell workers to invest as much in their retirement accounts as they can. We tell individuals to buy stocks priced low to then sell them high, yes, but we also say buy as much of that low-priced stock as you can. The language of debt is about minimizing. The language of investment is about maximizing. If you are investing in your future through education, through a powerful credential with symbolic value far beyond mere skill acquisition, you should invest big, not small.

I witnessed an online exchange among a group of women, all enrolled in a for-profit doctoral program, that demonstrated how they make sense of their education as an investment. Kristen shared a newspaper clipping about a former director of admissions at MIT who had been fired when it was discovered that she had lied about having a college degree. Marjorie, Valerie, Ellen, and Candice were livid at the implications. "As hard as I'm working for this degree and people out here LYIN' about having one!" Valerie said. Marjorie added, "I hope they make her pay back all the money she stole from them in salary," based, presumably, on the salary increase that comes with higher degree attainment. Candice shared a story about how this kind of "fraud" is happening so much that her employer had started randomly verifying the educational credentials of people that already worked there. "I tell them, you doubt? Just ask Sallie Mae." (Sallie Mae is a major student loan servicer.) Candice was intimating that her student loan payment was proof that she had a "real degree," unlike the fraud at MIT. Others chimed in, many laughing, saying that their debt was all the evidence they needed of their bona fides.

Taking on student loans as an investment rather than as a debt lent a kind of legitimacy for many of the students I talked to. Rather than a warning bell that a school might be somehow "not real" or illegitimate, the debt was proof that a school was a real school that offered real degrees—at real costs. Those real degrees, and the debt that came with them, represented the very real sacrifices students had made in earning them. It became a tangible marker of academic rigor, similar to the way students in traditional colleges might talk about passing a notoriously diffi-cult class that many have failed as evidence that their school is meritorious.

Swaggers did not see their debt as a moral crisis. Even when they struggled with finding more loan money because they had maxed out, they rarely blamed the high cost of their tuition. Instead, they shared resources on finding private student loans or getting exemptions for government loan programs for which they had been denied because of low credit scores. For example, Marjorie once asked for group support: "I have [almost maxed out on student loans and degree progress] due to going through seven [dissertation] Chairs and one committee member . . . there is not much support when Chairs and committee members disappear and/or give very little support." Tara offered support in the guise of the education gospel: "We all have been where you are once or twice while on the journey. You are not the first nor the last. God will send just what you need when you need it. Continue to lean on the people in this group." Marjorie told me later that the advice felt cloying. She was extremely stressed about finding the money to finish her own degree. She had invested three years and over $100,000 in pursuing it. Some Swaggers eventually offered Marjorie leads on a private student loan company. But most of the support reverted back to the functional good of struggling. Keisha offered, "Quitting is not an option" because the "community of doctors" is not for quitters.

Swaggers also discussed how others viewed their degrees, although, again, they rarely called their schools for-profit. Instead, they overwhelmingly used their school's name, and on a few occasions used "online schools." Rebecca talked about how someone at church made a snide comment ("threw shade") when she told them she was "doing [her] doctorate in leadership." I asked Rebecca why she thought the woman was dismissive. "Everybody don't understand the journey," she said. I asked if the woman had a degree. "I don't know. Probably. Yeah, I think so." Did she think that could have something to do with the disdain? Rebecca resisted explaining *why* the woman at church threw shade at her doctoral studies. Later, she returned to the topic to say that people who "went to school a long time ago" don't understand "how schools are now." That was the closest any of the Swaggers came to articulating an idea that their for-profit college was somehow different from traditional colleges, or that the differences might pose a problem for them.

The Swaggers may not have been comfortable talking about the prestige bias against their for-profit colleges, but they did share concerns about whether they would get a job. Fear about employability was the most common way Swaggers channeled ideas of prestige or inequality. In fact, I was surprised that a group where 68 percent of the members were black or black-mixed so rarely discussed race, gender, or inequality. I counted only one post that referenced race, and it was one celebrating "beautiful black women with dreams." However, four women ventured posts to express concerns that they wouldn't get a job with their doctorate degrees. Mary said:

> [I] would like to begin my PHD in October at ProfitU. I'm 46 years old and a little nervous that I will not be employable by the time I complete the program. Can some give me some advise [*sic*] or tell me about their experience at ProfitU or in the PHD program. Thanks.

Immediately, Swaggers exerted an alternative plausible explanation for Mary's concerns. Jada said, "First, you should not think you won't be employable. At that level, you create your own employment." Jada rejected any implications that any kind of inequality could undermine a degree. Other Swaggers agreed with and reinforced Jada's comment. And almost immediately, Swaggers resolved the issue by agreeing with Aubrey, who said, "If all else fails, start your own business." The takeaway was that Mary should not consider her doctorate degree to be an external object with objective labor market value. Instead, Mary should make sense of her educational pursuits as a process of becoming an entrepreneur.

When we spoke, one thing was clear: Mary did not want to start her own business. She had worked in education and for nonprofits for most of her professional career. As she got older, those working with her seemed to get younger. The status differences bothered Mary. "I need to stay [at her current level of employment] or get higher. I'm too old to go *down*," she said. Mary had worked her way through a bachelor's degree completion program in her thirties. She had thought she was finished. Then she got a master's at forty-one when her employer offered to pay for most of it and she was guaranteed a salary increase upon completion. She was subsequently laid off from her job at a school, and the nonprofit market seemed to have moved beyond her master's credentials. At least in education nonprofits, it seemed to Mary like "everyone is a doctor!" Even younger workers were doctors, requiring Mary to use the honorific "doctor" when addressing people who either worked for her or had less work experience than she did. "People just act different when you have a title," she said. When I asked Mary if she was planning to enroll in the program, she told me that she had just done so that week. She didn't sound confident about her prospects, but she did say, more than once, "They can't take your education from you."

For-profit colleges organize their entire enrollment process to catch Mary in a moment of weakness when she has spent the day calling someone twenty years her junior "doctor." I focus on the Swaggers because discussions of for-profit colleges' recruitment strategies too often assume a low-information prospect with little support. And while there is certainly some truth to that dynamic, it doesn't account for or explain people like the Swaggers who are, as graduate degree seekers, by definition not exactly low-information. Some Swaggers had traditional undergraduate or master's degrees. They were savvy enough to share information about navigating private and federal student loan underwriting criteria. Others had formed social networks with other educated people, presumably broadening their access to cultural capital. Yet the enrollment process that generated so much revenue for shareholder for-profit colleges, making the Wall Street era the most profitable in Lower Ed's history, still worked for the Swaggers.

Swaggers told me that their options for graduate study were few. They said they wanted the degree even if it did not lead to a job, because the social status attached to the credential was worth their investment. They also talked about changes in work that were impacting even educated, middle-class Americans, especially women. In the fields of education, healthcare, nonprofit occupational areas, and in other jobs where women have made particularly strong inroads, maintaining their career level or moving to a higher one meant getting another degree. Far from being shocked by the high debt they had taken on to get that degree, Swaggers understood the debt as a symbol of quality. Remember, not even employers and accreditation agencies can agree on how to define quality.

Swaggers aren't alone in being unsure or agnostic about traditional symbols of higher education quality: one-on-one instruction, prestige of professors, library holdings, and fancy buildings. Until the Wall Street era of for-profit colleges, price was a fairly good proxy for institutional prestige. A good college was generally a more expensive one. A less expensive college was generally less prestigious. Only with the rapid rise of for-profit colleges and their expansion into upmarket degrees did price become decoupled from prestige. In the 2000s, suddenly the most expensive colleges were the least prestigious ones. When time is a valuable commodity for the likely for-profit college student, and revenues are derived almost entirely from enrollment, the least prestigious colleges enroll students quickly—leaving them to make sense of it all only after they have invested a significant amount into the enterprise.

5

WHERE CREDIT IS DUE

One of the greatest purported strengths of the U.S. higher education system is the ability to move in and out of it over time and throughout changing life circumstances. It is not the statistically likely story, but in the United States it is possible to drop out of high school, later earn a diploma by taking the general equivalency degree (GED) exam, go to a community college, transfer to a four-year college, and go on to high-status graduate and professional schools to earn a master's and even a doctoral degree.

In 2014, I sat down to talk to Kevin Golembiewski. Kevin is a junior partner in a Philadelphia law firm. He specializes in civil rights and education law. As a graduate of Harvard Law School and a young, fit, attractive white male to boot, it's a career choice among many possible options for Kevin. He could have joined his peers at corporate law firms in New York City, enabling him to buy and sell a college professor a few times over in just a few short years. Instead, Kevin opted for a more modest salary and a job with a mission to serve the public good. It may have something to do with where Kevin started out.

A year before we met, Kevin wrote an op-ed for a public policy blog about how he started his educational career at a community college. In the op-ed, he argues that his unlikely trajectory is proof that substantial investment in public higher education can pay off. When we talked, the first thing I wanted to know is how a kid from a Florida community college makes it to Harvard Law School. Kevin starts with the one word that wasn't in his op-ed and is rarely uttered in the Horatio Alger public policy that eats up his kind of personal story with a gilded spoon. "Luck. My story was a lot of luck," Kevin tells me.

Although he grew up "mostly poor," for a few years he lived in a wealthier neighborhood when his mother entered a new relationship. There he made friends like the one whose father would eventually take an interest in Kevin's well-being. Kevin remembers that applying to college felt like a crapshoot. There were things that people where he was from in Florida "just did," like pining for admissions to Florida State University. If you could not get into or afford Florida State University, you went to a local community college. Someone Kevin can't remember came to his school once and helped him complete financial aid paperwork. He doesn't remember knowing anything about institutional aid, and thought you only got scholarships from playing sports. Institutional aid is how wealthy schools with deep endowments discount the sticker price of their tuition for students. Through a combination of grants and scholarships, some of the most elite colleges can be comparable in price to less expensive public colleges. The trick is that you have to apply to know it is an option—unless, of course, you have a cultural liaison to decode a process that is deliberately obtuse to outsiders like Kevin.

Kevin applied to Florida State and the University of Arizona; the former because it was what one did and the latter because he had been born in Arizona. After looking at the tuition costs of both, Kevin decided to go to community college. In his essay, Kevin describes the experience as one veiled in shame: "You only end up in community college if you're lazy or not good enough for real college." As several friends pulled away, stratified by the prestige of their college institutions, one friendship yielded unexpected fruit that would change the course of Kevin's life.

The stint his family did in the wealthy neighborhood put Kevin's world on a crash course with a friend's dad, whom Kevin alternately calls his sponsor and mentor. This friend's dad thought Kevin too smart for "just" community college. With his own son away at an elite school in the northeast, Kevin's mentor knew the game of college admissions. He explained things like institutional aid and "small liberal arts colleges," knowledge previously unknown to Kevin. After two years at community college, Kevin transferred to the private College of the Holy Cross. "It's not an Ivy, but it was a world away from community college," Kevin says. I ask him to think back to the transfer process, because that is where college trajectories from low-prestige institutions to high-prestige institutions either become grist for the mill or grind the gears of mobility to a sudden halt. Did anyone help him with the mechanics of credit hour transfers? "You mean like explain it all to me or anything? No. But I remember the guidance counselor [at Holy Cross] telling me that almost no one has all their credits transfer in. Mine did."

Kevin isn't sure why all his credit hours transferred. He cannot recall ever meeting anyone else at Holy Cross who began at a community college. There isn't much reason to believe that the reputation of his Florida community college had smoothed the way. What Kevin does know is that the transfer hours saved him time and money. "If I would have had to start over . . . I guess I would have, but only because I owed my mentor and I would have done anything he told me to do. But it would have negated the entire cost-saving benefit" that had been part of the reason that he chose a community college to begin with.

Over time, Kevin was not from a community college so much as he was from Holy Cross. His application to Harvard lacked the prestige he knows is "heavily weighted in admissions," but a small, private, liberal arts education had provided him the letters of recommendation, know-how, and standing to gain admission to Harvard Law School. "There was so much change in my life in just six or seven years that I'm still processing it really." The change is not all easy. There's the cultural conflict of new social norms. There's learning a new language of class and privilege and wealth. There's overcoming the shame of how you started to develop "the swagger you need in law school," as Kevin describes it.

For all the discomfort, the rewards are significant. Kevin struggles to put words to the experience of how all that wealth and prestige manifests day to day: "The people you meet, I mean . . ." Kevin doesn't finish the sentence, and his voice fades away. He trusts that I know what he means. I'm an outsider, too. I know that feeling, he is saying to me. And he is right. The first time I attended a recruiting event for a graduate program it was at Duke University. I remember looking around the room at all the pale faces, bluntly cut bangs, and those garish quilted bags and thinking I had fallen through the looking glass. These were people like me, yet not at all like me. These were the people you meet that Kevin cannot describe. And meeting them can change your life for the better and for the worse, often doing both at the same time.

Kevin is Exhibit A for the open, porous U.S. system of higher education. Recently, I gave a talk in which I mentioned my concerns about the privatization of the general equivalency degree (GED) program. Privatizing the GED had made it more expensive and more dependent on having things like Internet access and computer skills. In 2013, after the GED was sold to for-profit Pearson Education, several states reported declines in pass rates and test taking. The GED is one of those porous points in the structure of U.S. higher education, like community college. A man from New Zealand was in the audience and asked me, befuddled, what did I mean by an equivalency exam. After I explained it, he continued to struggle with a culturally relevant analogy. "You mean," he finally said, "you can drop out of high school and . . . come back?" He was confused because in almost no other system in the world is that as possible.

In countries with what sociologists call a strong structure of education, when you get out of the pipeline that carries students from primary school to tertiary or post-secondary education, you are out. There's no testing your way back in. That system makes for amazing rates of achievement . . . for those who do not exit the system. In contrast, our system says hard work—and luck—can put you back in a pipeline that could even possibly take you all the way to Harvard, the Shangri-la of U.S. higher education. Kevin's story is the story of how our system of higher education is unique by being structured to allow this sort of opportunity. Of course, the opportunity is not perfect. It still requires more luck than hard work—and it requires a lot of hard work. And, for certain, the opportunity is not evenly distributed. "A lot of people liked me along the way, professors and teachers. But I was a white guy. If I had been black or, like, a black woman, I don't know if that would have been the same," Kevin says.

Research shows that empathy, the kind that a professor or a benefactor acts on when a student reminds her of her son or herself years ago, is racialized. Racial empathy gaps in pain have been observed in numerous studies. The takeaway is that across race people are more empathetic toward whites, more likely to feel their perceived pain, and, presumably, more inclined to act to mitigate that pain.[1] Whether the pain was physical or emotional, when Kevin's benefactor looked at him, he empathized with this smart kid making a bad educational choice. So he intervened. That his intervention was even possible, however, is because Kevin was able to transfer his college credits and gain the opportunity facilitated by that one seemingly simple action. It's what people and policy makers mean when they talk about higher education "access" as being critical to social mobility.

One of the enduring narratives of for-profit colleges is that they expand access to higher education. Should life circumstances force a student to withdraw from school, for-profit colleges are said to be a way back into the system of transferability and possibility. That ideology does not match the empirical reality. Transfer credit is not a sexy-sounding topic, but it is an important part of understanding how porous the structure of higher education is and is not for students in for-profit colleges.

A National Center of Education Statistics (NCES) report took up the question of transfer credits.[2] It found that of students in degree-eligible programs (meaning not those in programs that offer short-term certificates in either the public or for-profit sector), for-profit students transferred the least. The lowest percentages of students transferring or simultaneously enrolling in more than one school were for those in less-than-four-year for-profit colleges, and those in four-year for-profits. More students lost credits they had earned when they moved from public to private for-profit institutions and from private not-for-profits than to any other type of institution (69 percent and 83 percent respectively) when compared to students moving from public to other public institutions (38 percent).

If you have ever transferred into or out of any college program, you know that you often lose credits, even if the receiving institution allows some of your credits to transfer. Credit loss is about two precious resources that most students, especially for-profit students, have in short supply: time and money. More transfer credits means not repeating coursework and finishing a degree program sooner. Finishing a degree program sooner can mean paying less in tuition. On the issue of credit loss, the same NCES report found that most students lose hours when transferring, but "credit loss for students transferring out of for-profit institutions ranged from 17 to 25 credits." That is more credit loss than that experienced by those in private traditional colleges (the researchers could not make a comparable measure for credit loss in the public traditional college sector due to data and measurement issues). The following table is a summary of transfer activity among students by the type of school and its sector. It captures transfer activity between 2003 and 2009, which is part of a significant period of growth in for-profit college enrollment.

Table 5.1

The percentage distribution and number of all potential transfer opportunities among first-time beginning undergraduate students who transferred/coenrolled, by control, level, sector, and accreditation relationship: 2003–04 to 2008–09

Institutional relationship	Percent of transfer opportunities	Number of transfer/ coenrollment events (thousands)
Total	**100.0**	**2,604**
Control		
Public to public	64.4	1,680
Public to private non-profit	13.3	347
Public to private for-profit	4.3	113
Private non-profit to public	9.4	245
Private non-profit to private non-profit	3.1	81
Private non-profit to private for-profit	0.5	13
Private for-profit to public	3.0	78
Private for-profit to private non-profit	0.4	11
Private for-profit to private for-profit	1.6	41

Source: National Center for Education Statistics

Transferring is a hot topic among those who talk about for-profit colleges for a living. In 2011, my colleagues and I convened a conference at Duke University on for-profit higher education. From the outset, I did not want the event to turn into a dialectical war of "profit is bad"/"public is good" ideologies. Those are fun, but they are not very useful for students who 1) do not demonstrate much awareness of "for-profit" as a designation; 2) think college is college; and 3) choose among colleges in only the most precise definition of the word. I sent out invitations to every email address for for-profit college executives that I could mine from the Internet. I was pleasantly surprised by the positive response. My only stipulations were that participants had to pay for their own travel (doing what little I could to stem the transfer of public money to the market!) and they had to stay for the whole event. No dropping in and out. I wanted engagement. I wanted to signal to my traditional college colleagues that we ignore the for-profit college sector as partners at our own peril. We are, like the students making those enrollment choices every day amid shifting and difficult circumstances, all in this together. In the end, five of the nation's largest for-profit colleges were represented at the conference.

I went into the event expecting to do a fair amount of refereeing. At the time, congressional debates were being had about changes to the regulation of for-profits. The media cycle on for-profit colleges had picked up steam. New media and traditional media outlets were suddenly dedicating real resources to covering higher education as a distinct beat. Once resources have been allocated to cover news of a phenomenon, they will make a phenomenon of any news. States were signaling that they would start exerting more regulation over for-profit colleges that were conferring degrees within their borders. To my surprise, when the topics I thought most contentious came up—Congress, regulation, the gainful employment rule—there was little rancor. The for-profit college executives looked mostly resigned, if not comfortable, with those topics of discussion.

The topic I had not anticipated to be contentious was credit transfers. When a traditional college researcher casually mentioned that we should think about whether for-profit students can transfer to a "real school," the room erupted. I use eruption here in the erudite, high-culture version of the word. There were no fist fights or profanity. But the energy in the room ratcheted up discernably. Voices were raised. A collective outburst from most of the for-profit college executives in response signaled that we had entered contested territory. One executive pointed out that many for-profit colleges have articulation agreements with traditional colleges in their geographic region. He was correct. Education researchers have studied articulation agreements for years, particularly in studies of the community college sector, because their mission to create access makes those agreements salient. Policy analysts Gregory Anderson, Jeffrey Sun, and Mariana Alfonso say that "articulation agreements serve to negotiate the requirements for students' movement from institution to institution and support the transfer intent." [3]

In articulation agreements, institutions get together and pinky swear to allow students with certain types of credits for courses taken at their respective institutions to port those credits fairly easily. But like any good pinky-swear, it takes two pinkies to tango. Both institutions must meet at the table, agree to the terms, and then honor them. For-profit colleges like Argosy were touting their articulation agreements with traditional not-for-profit colleges to potential investors in their investment prospectuses. Most of the action in cross-sector articulation agreements has happened between for-profits and community colleges. Kaplan announces its articulation agreements with community colleges on its website, promising that transfer credits are a great way to save money and time. [4]

Articulation agreements sound like a great boon for students, especially students for whom social inequality and changes in the labor market make it necessary to do school on the metaphorical second or third shift. But articulation agreements are about more than convenience. Another for-profit college executive in the room condemned people "like you," meaning those of us from traditional elite higher education, for refusing to extend a pinky for articulation agreements. He was not entirely wrong. Think of it like a college sports conference. Many schools play teams that are nowhere near them geographically but that are perceived as being close to them in prestige. Sociologist Mitchell Stevens describes a small liberal arts college's spending a lot of money to ship its lacrosse team across the country to play. Collegiate sports conferences are a way of saying, "This is who we are relative to who our institutional peers are." And because the vast majority of the public will never attend an elite college, and only in recent history has a slight majority attended any college at all, collegiate leagues are an implicit signal of prestige. It is why my dear old alma mater, a public historically black college in North Carolina, left the traditionally black Central Intercollegiate Athletic Association league in 2009, to the dismay of many. It joined the league that allows its teams, for example, to play the University of North Carolina as opposed to Bethune Cookman College. That you have probably heard of UNC and not Bethune Cookman is why a school might spend so much money, political will, and energy to make such a switch.

Articulation agreements are first, genuinely, and most ostensibly about maintaining curriculum quality. I do not want to argue differently. But just like going to the Final Four is about more than athletic pride, articulation agreements also signal peerage. If the courses that are earned at another institution are equivalent in content—and, more importantly (and most amorphously), quality—then by what measure does an entire subsector in education differentiate itself? For community colleges, who still rely greatly on geographic proximity to define the students they serve, this question is not of much concern. If a student moves closer to another college, there are still plenty of students left in the area to serve. Also, the access mission of community colleges means that generally they will eventually adapt to serve the students that are close to them. However, in the competitive game of four-year colleges, especially those among the most elite, attracting students is about more than proximity and access. It is also about reputation and prestige. This leads to the most elite schools having some of the most strident anti-transfer policies.

In 2011, the *Harvard Crimson* reported a "minuscule 1 percent—that was the admissions rate for transfer students last year after Harvard decided to accept just 15 students of the 1,486 who applied to transfer to the college." Yale advertises that it has only "20 to 30 spots for transfer students" per year. In 2012, the school admitted five such students. But Harvard and Yale do better than Princeton, which accepts no transfer students as a matter of policy. There is a case—albeit an elitist one—that these institutions are simply without peers. To do well in their environments, students must be inculcated into their high-quality curriculums from the start. Moreover, these institutions have a serious vested interest in producing exclusive degrees. When those scrolls bear the name Harvard, Yale, or Princeton, they must mean that and that alone.

But all colleges are not Harvard, Yale, and Princeton—a fact that many of us should be happy about. Why would a state public college not extend articulation agreements to for-profit colleges, especially if doing so would open up that porous structure I described earlier? There are several reasons. First, traditional colleges of all prestige levels have serious concerns about the quality of courses at for-profit colleges. Some of this is about elitism, but, again, we endeavor to be fair and critical in the disciplined meaning of the word. The fact is, for-profit colleges have not done much to pull back the curtain on their classrooms. They frequently cite market competiveness as a concern when publishing research findings about proprietary curriculum, labor arrangements, and organizational processes. Since faculty at for-profit colleges are rarely expected to conduct research as part of their job duties, we do not learn about for-profits the way we have learned so much about traditional colleges. Traditional college faculty must publish or perish, and students are convenient study populations. Some researchers have gained on-campus access to observe for-profit colleges in action, but that is relatively privileged access. Indeed, one aim of the conference at Duke was to foster our own kind of research articulation agreements that would allow traditional researchers access to for-profit college campuses and processes. Those seeds are now growing and bearing slow, slow fruit.[5]

An increase in political scrutiny has made for-profit colleges, and particularly their corporate superiors, sensitive to outside research attempts.

Another reason traditional colleges have been slow to develop articulation agreements with for-profit colleges is because we may not all be Harvard, Yale, or Princeton, but many of us want to be. Traditional higher education, if we think of it as a market (though I am not a fan of doing so), does not just market education and degrees. It also markets prestige. How often have you, possessor of a college degree of any kind, actually been asked to perform any of the skills your resume says you possess when you apply for a job? I suspect it has happened rarely. Degrees do as much signaling as they do certifying. That is, they certify a set of skills, surely, but they also signal a set of behaviors to recruitment agents. Those agents work in organizations that have spent decades developing systems based on the notion that degrees signal certain abilities, traits, and behaviors. There are few recruitment processes designed to test what an applicant really knows or can really do.

Colleges, like the "WannabeUs" or universities that Gaye Tuchman describes in her book, *Wannabe U*, are very sensitive to anything that might compromise the perceived value of their credentials as signals for important stakeholders—political bodies, accreditors, prospective students, and, yes, recruitment agents. Tuchman describes WannabeUs as schools with more resources than prestige that are driven to increase their institutional standing among aspirational peer institutions. Eponymous rankings like those by the *U.S. News and World Report* annual lists drive WannabeUs' aspirations and become the measure by which their success is judged.[6]

It should be noted that until 2010, USNWR had never ranked for-profit colleges. In its 2009 rankings the venerable college rankings publication said that no such colleges had yet conformed to the methodology. According to one of the most powerful tertiary agencies in higher education, for-profit colleges were no one's peers, aspirational or otherwise. Traditional colleges and universities, besieged by declining state subsidies and changing political attitudes about the value of higher education, may better serve students by initiating articulation agreements with for-profit colleges. But, they do so at the risk of also validating the perceived value of the degrees for-profits confer to students. For the for-profits, these articulation gaps simply create more profit potential.

At the time that it went public in 2006, Argosy said it was the "largest for-profit provider of doctoral degrees." The corporate entity also owned other schools that offered certificates, associate's degrees, and bachelor's degrees. Speaking to the SEC's regulations and to potential investors, Argosy made a clear statement on the value of pipelines, or credentialing sequences, as a financial strength. By buying and strengthening its presence in the realm of sub-graduate degree programs, the "company can also take advantage of the tendency of many graduates of master's, bachelor's and associate degree programs to continue their education at the same institution if appropriate advanced degree programs are offered." To students, all this political economy of prestige, pinky swears, and rankings is mostly invisible. Even when they bump up against the constraints of transferability and credit portability, students have no means of judging the complex web that ensnares their educational aspirations.

Raley is a first-generation college student. She did not just make it to college; she made it to an Ivy League college. She is African American and funny. I know this because I followed her lifestyle and news blog for several years. It swings between essays on getting a perfectly smooth ponytail to the representation of black women in popular culture. I knew her in the sense that we know people these days in 140-character tweets, 450-word blog posts, and gifs, avatars, and follow-backs. Raley emailed me one day asking for a favor. It turns out she knew me, too. She knew that

I tweet and write a lot about for-profit colleges. For a few weeks we exchanged emails and phone calls, and the way we knew one another changed.

Raley's mother had gone back to school during Raley's sophomore year in college. She had enrolled in a for-profit college. She was now close to "maxing out," or exceeding the aggregate total federal student aid limits, but she had not yet finished earning her degree. Raley wondered if I had some advice. I have had this conversation maybe 250 times now with people on buses, with administrative assistants in the office of my university, audience members, and random readers and tweeters who do not know me at all. Sometimes they are asking for themselves, but overwhelmingly they are asking for a family member. My favorite instance is the time one of my dissertation advisers emailed me about his sister-in-law, because it showed just how porous our social worlds can be. Sometimes the questions are about how to get into school. Sometimes the questions are about how to get out of school. Nearly every time, the event that prompts a call, an email, a tug on my sleeve at a conference is something about money. They've run out, are about to run out, just got a statement from a place they don't know by name about how much they'll soon have to pay. Or someone told them that their school costs too much.

Raley wanted to know what her mom should do. After a decade of experience, research, and thinking about questions precisely like this, I still do not have a good answer. I will share what I told Raley and her mother, my best friend's mother's best friend, my adviser to tell his sister-in-law, and the woman on the number 9 bus in Atlanta about her son. I will write about it here because it is, in part, about articulation and credit transferability and prestige.

If a student is close to graduating and close to maxing out, I believe any credential is preferable to no credential. The time and energy invested in those for-profit credits are—as we've seen—not often transferred into less expensive traditional colleges at rates that offset the tuition savings. Losing thirty credits can be equivalent to a year if you were or are attending school full-time, longer if you are not. My next point is more complicated now that I have written about the labor market reception to for-profit credentials, but remember the ways of recruitment agents, organizational processes, and how you apply for a job. Sometimes all you need is to be able to check the box that says "college" next to "highest education finished" to move along in a hiring process. These processes are increasingly automated and are often calibrated to winnow very large pools of applicants, especially since technology has made it easier to apply to a lot of jobs indiscriminately. Of course, this is also a signal of a job market with more people competing for jobs. But let us keep this specific for now.

For individuals, especially those who have an "ethnic name," a baby bump, or a dearth of elite social contacts, being able to check that box still matters. I'd argue that this is true even if the degree is from a for-profit college. I hypothesize that it is even *more* true when you are applying to large bureaucracies or public-sector jobs that have rigid, formal hiring protocols and are sensitive to anti-discrimination regulations. If you are maxing out and close to finishing the degree, leave with the degree. I went on to tell Raley and her mother that the calculus is different earlier on in your education. If you want to transfer out a year or so into a for-profit college degree program, I think the math of student aid—and the math of life—is in your favor. You have less time and money invested. Evidence shows that you may have better outcomes with that other degree. Important to note is that when you transfer, you must be emotionally prepared for losing credits.

That moment when you have worked so hard and done all the right things only to learn that at your new school none of it will matter is what undermined London when she tried to leave Everest College. Far too often our statistical models and methods for analyzing what happens in higher ed understate the emotional toil of educational aspirations. Starting from scratch because articulation agreements and credit transfers and financial aid regulations negate the effort you've expended is a real human cost. Despite knowing me far better than Raley or the lady on the bus did, London stayed at Everest College even as bankruptcy rumors about the school swirled, her math courses stymied her degree progress, and her student loan debt mounted. I could not help London. She was in too deep, too far from where she had started, and not close enough to finish relative to how much she already owed. Because our families are close, I told her the truth that I never, ever, ever drop on strangers on buses or online friends via email: there is no good resolution to that problem.

6

CREDENTIALS, JOBS, AND THE NEW ECONOMY

In 2014, I was a research fellow at the Center for Poverty Research at the University of California, Davis. I had proposed a policy-oriented paper about the link between welfare reform and short-term occupational certificates. You may recall that the nation ended "welfare as we know it," according to then president Bill Clinton, when he signed into law the most sweeping changes to anti-poverty programs in almost half a century. It was 1996 and the name change said it all. The Aid to Families with Dependent Children (AFDC) programs were replaced with Temporary Assistance for Needy Families (TANF). The major changes were to how what we colloquially call welfare would be funded and administered. The other part of the act—the Personal Responsibility and Work Opportunity Reconciliation Act (PRWORA)—had a piece I thought was key to understanding how people in tough economic circumstances find their way to costly for-profit colleges.

In short, states adopted—piecemeal or wholesale—various work requirements for those seeking public assistance. Many of these requirements included a provision for "participating in an educational occupational training program" like those we offered at the Beauty College. On a weekly basis, I completed verification documents for women who were on public assistance. The forms verified the hours that they were in class. I also helped students when they needed additional documentation to get childcare subsidies, like discounted daycare rates. This support with paperwork was vital to enrolling students at the Beauty College and to keeping them enrolled. We relied on our students' ability to come to class to earn their "clock hours," the time they were physically present in class. Our majority female student body relied on a patchwork of social services to be able to attend class and earn their clock hours. Both course schedules—one day and one evening—overlapped with the typical K–12 school day and the important afterschool gap that most parents are familiar with. (If a typical school day for your children ends at 3 p.m. and a workday ends at 5 p.m. if you're lucky, 7 p.m. if you're not, or at no consistent time at all [variable work shifts], what do you do with your children?)

In many ways the students at the Beauty College who qualified for daycare subsidies had the better of available options, as Aaron had pointed out. The students who did not qualify for or did not participate in those programs relied heavily on partners, families, and friends to help them care for school-age children. They were often also the students who took longer over a calendar year to earn enough clock hours to graduate. Because I had participated at the periphery of these complex institutional connections—public schools, daycare, welfare programs, and for-profit colleges—I grew curious about what kind of schools the millions of people who needed welfare programs ended up enrolling in and why. I was especially interested in what kinds of messages those in the welfare system got from caseworkers and peers about what schools to go to. I wondered if they were like Mike, swimming in the calmer stream of the for-profit college river, getting messages about a hustle that made enrolling at a for-profit a better fit than a community college or other public school.

With forty-five interviews with for-profit college students under my belt and a dozen with faculty members at for-profit colleges, I was well situated to tackle this question. I'd met with executives from all but two of the nation's largest shareholder for-profit colleges by this point. I had developed a small reputation of being fair. At least that's what the executive of one for-profit college told me: "I know we might not ever agree, Tressie, but you are *fair.*" Lawrence was a small-town boy from the South. He had worked his way through traditional colleges and knew how hard that was to do. He was deeply disturbed by the rhetoric in higher education circles about poor students, older students, and rural students—people who reminded him of his younger self. More than any executive at any for-profit college I met with save for one, Lawrence made me believe that *he* believed his mission at a for-profit college was serving the greater public good. "Our students aren't stupid, Tressie," he'd say to me time and time again.

I believed him. I knew students in for-profit colleges were not stupid. It chaps my hide to this day that academics at elite institutions talk about a significant proportion of students in higher education as gullible sheep with low cognitive abilities. Lawrence knew my position on profit-generating, private-sector, occupationally oriented credentials differed from his. But he also trusted that I shared his commitment to students. After a year of ongoing dialogue, Lawrence offered me unprecedented access to his company's brand of (mostly) certificate-granting colleges in California during my time at UC Davis.

We agreed that I would have access to students and facilities without a liaison present. This was major, as my previous access to other for-profit colleges had always stipulated constant oversight. We were clear that my notes and any write-ups would not be "vetted" by anyone at the company. They asked only that I share those write-ups with them. That seemed fair, or certainly as fair as any deal I'd ever gotten from a for-profit school. Because this is a private-sector entity, the institution did not have a formal review process for me to complete, but I did complete the one at my own institution. I spoke with several of the local school directors, wrote up my interview guides, and prepared to observe.

The day of my first scheduled appointment I woke up to three

emails from various people about "for-profit colleges in California."
As I'd slept with visions of research stardom dancing in my head,
the California state attorney general had executed search warrants
and announced a lawsuit was being filed against the company
where I was doing my research. Once they had far bigger fish to fry,
my access to the college dried up, and I moved on to research local
community colleges and a for-profit college that served the area's
large military population. I would follow the California lawsuits
for over two years. The attorney general was young and ambitious.
The case seemed poised to make her a political star, and her narrative was clear: this chain of for-profit colleges had fraudulently
enrolled students using phony job-placement rates.

All affection for Lawrence aside, I do not doubt the claim. It
is just far too easy to misrepresent job-placement and labor market data. At the Beauty College, we were issued new sheets with
bright, colorful infographics about data on the "cosmetology profession" once a year. They had income projections from the Bureau
of Labor Statistics (BLS). Cosmetology professionals, we told prospective students, could make $38,000 a year. The field, we said,
was projected to grow over the coming decade. At the Technical
College, we had similar infographics, also from the BLS. There,
the projections were even more favorable and used words like
"high growth," "in demand," and "professional." The technical
industry was the wave of the future, and technical professionals,
from engineers to tech-savvy criminal justice professionals, could
command high salaries, respect, and mobility.

When I returned to for-profit colleges to study the enrollment
process as detailed in Chapter 4, I found that the infographics
had not changed much. Each of the schools I visited and enrolled
in still used BLS data with income and labor market growth
data. Each of them had asterisks with small print about the data
not indicating a promise of labor market returns. Each of them
made a big deal—through design and the enrollment counselors'
presentation—about the data being from the federal government

and not something made up at the school. Job-placement data for
the actual school was usually included in the information packet.
These data were always subordinated to BLS data. The BLS data
usually included colorful infographics and very large fonts, whereas
the job-placement data was generally in a footnote or small table.
The implication from the materials was clear: national job projections were more important than the school's job-placement performance. Enrollment officers drew explicit connections between
labor market statistics about the fastest growing careers and the
degree programs offered at the college. EOs frequently described
these careers in qualitative status terms. For example, when enrolling at ITT Technical Institute I was told that technology jobs
were "more professional" and you could "go anywhere" with a degree in technology. This tapped into narratives of social mobility
that ran throughout the education gospel, but also into assumptions about precarious employment—specifically that it is low-
status work with few paths to promotion over time.

Capella University also pointed out that a degree in business
could lead to better-quality work and that eventually I might pursue a master's in business administration to be really immune to labor market vicissitudes. The enrollment officer said that graduate
degrees afford more job security. At American Intercontinental
University, the enrollment officer asked particularly pointed questions about my current work. When I told her that my current
work does not allow a set schedule, she nodded enthusiastically
and said that a more professional career comes with better, standardized hours as well as better pay.

The labor projections at each of the schools—and the projections I once shared with prospective students—are a version of the
truth. Cosmetology professionals *can* earn as much as $38,000 a
year, but the median income for them is $23,710 a year, or $11.40
an hour.[1] Computer programmers with a bachelor's degree *can*
earn $79,530 a year, as 2015 BLS data and projections shared at
tech-orientated for-profit colleges indicate. The data seem like

promises even when enrollment counselors are clear to point out that they are not. The data have the weight of the U.S. government behind them. The data are concrete. But, like any data, they can tell vastly different stories depending on the other data at your disposal and your ability to extrapolate from numbers to experience. For example, the BLS also has data on cosmetology earnings by industry, but that data isn't listed on the infographics provided to prospective students at any of the beauty colleges I worked for or visited. Looking at differences by industry offers a more nuanced perspective because it puts the numbers in context. Top earners in the cosmetology profession work in "performing arts companies" like those in Hollywood, yes, but also like cruise ship lines. Cosmetologists in this entertainment industry have an annual average salary of $64,580, or $31.05 an hour. These are highly competitive positions with difficult points of entry. At the lower end of salaries, cosmetologists work in "personal care services" like national chain salons—places like the Hair Cuttery, Supercuts, or Best Cuts—or even in retirement homes and funeral homes. In that part of the industry, a licensed cosmetologist earns $27,860 a year, or $13.40 an hour. Remember, in the 2000s those students were paying approximately $15,000 for a nine-month certificate at the Beauty College. In 2014 when I visited a similar beauty college in a suburb of Atlanta, the tuition was $21,436.[2]

Almost 97 percent of students in for-profit college certificate programs use federal student aid to pay their tuition. Assuming a student does not qualify for "free" grant money (such as the Pell grant) and borrows the full cost of tuition to attend the Beauty College, they would have a $246 monthly loan payment on an anticipated wage of $13.40 an hour, or approximately $2,100 in gross monthly income (before taxes) on a full-time schedule. A lot goes into deciding the value of that credential given those numbers: whether that student loan payment is the student's only debt burden; the cost of basic living expenses, including housing and food; and any childcare costs. Let's look at some student data again. If 67 percent of the students enrolled in for-profit college certificate programs are poor enough to qualify for need-based grants, which they are, then they are likely living at or near the poverty line. There isn't good data on students in the for-profit college sector over the course of their lives, or much qualitative data on their experience of tuition and debt, but we do know more than a bit about living at or near the poverty line.

We know that the majority of Americans will be poor at some point in their lives. To talk about poverty is to talk about ourselves at some point in our lives. We know that relatively small amounts of money can make a big difference when you are poor or near poor. Having the $400 when your car breaks down instead of having it two weeks after your car breaks down can make the difference in your ability to keep the job that keeps you afloat. Not having that money when you need it can start a death spiral into debt and deprivation. We know that any lump sum income when you are poor or near poverty is usually used to dig one's self out of a hole created by the moments when you didn't have on-demand cash but needed it. We know that decision making skews toward short-term decisions when you are poor or near poor. Long-term planning, be it financial planning or educational planning, is a luxury born of means. We also know that one's relationship to money and debt is different when one has been poor, is poor, or fears becoming poor again. You may value monthly payments over the amortized costs of a loan over ten years, for instance. Or you may value financing your curling irons over paying cash for them. All of these conditions of poverty and near poverty are well documented. It is quite reasonable to assume that these conditions do not evaporate when one picks up the phone to call a for-profit college.

Students at for-profit colleges are more likely than students at traditional colleges to be impacted by constrained choices because of who they are and what they do (or do not) have, things like money and time. Alternatively, enrollment counselors are not actually counselors but rather are a sales force, as Lisa had frequently told me at the Technical College. Counseling might include providing context for job data. It might include information on student loan repayments and loan burdens. It might end with suggesting the community college across town, if it is a better fit. A sales force, however, is obligated to operate only up to the letter of a regulation, not its spirit. That translates to providing job-placement data because the Department of Education requires it, but not going so far as to complicate the data with its context. The structure of a college as a profit-generating business fetishizes efficiencies. Infographics are efficient. Counseling, especially the competent good kind, is individualized and inefficient. For students, the enrollment process can be faster and more flexible as a result, but it can also be more expensive with respect to time and money in the long term. Presently, there is no mechanism for resolving that tension.

I was never able to conduct my study of welfare programs at the for-profit college after the State Bureau of Investigators closed my field site. Some researchers have found quantitative links between changes in welfare policies and enrollment in short-term credential programs, the sort that for-profit colleges dominate. Historically, workforce credentialing programs were rife with public- and private-sector graft. One researcher, Regina Werum, documents the early twentieth-century analog to certificate programs. Werum essentially finds the same relationship that Sara Goldrick-Rab finds in a study conducted on late twentieth- and early twenty-first-century programs. The gist of these studies is that the context in which credentialing programs operate matters.

The context of the Wall Street era of for-profit college expansion is the new economy, an economy that is markedly distinct from the one that buoyed the social contract between labor, education, and work during public higher education's golden era of expansion in the mid-1900s. In this context, Lawrence is right: for-profit college students are far from stupid. However, Lawrence is more generous about the cynicism of for-profit colleges than am I. Any way you slice it, the quintessential for-profit college type of the past few decades (the sector's most expansive historical period to date) has identified and aggressively targeted the weaknesses of the context (the new economy) in which higher education credentials are earned. Workers are caught in the crosshairs, and all we have managed to give them is more infographics with BLS data.

When people talk about for-profit colleges, they often do so with a lot of disdain. If traditional colleges that take in a fraction of willing students every year annoy you, then you might be disdainful of their "prestige cartel." If you are concerned about vulnerable people making expensive educational decisions with little information, then you might disdain the "predatory" for-profit schools. If you think that a strong work ethic can trump all manner of troubles, you might disdain the "weak" people who go to a "predatory" school. What is interesting to me is how much disdain is spread among students and schools and how little disdain there is for labor markets. More than any other kind of college in the United States, for-profit colleges are judged by their ability to get their students jobs. Sure, the Department of Education's career programs in community colleges are held to the same job-placement guidelines as career programs are in for-profit colleges. Yet it is almost inconceivable to think about shuttering a community college.

Take, for example, City College of San Francisco. Writer Haley Sweetland Edwards once called it "America's Worst Community College."[3] By 2010, California's once sterling reputation for public support of higher education was showing deep fiscal fissures. With the downward trend in investment, so went community colleges' graduation rate, down 9.5 percent in eight years (2002–2010). Edwards doesn't account for the difficulties we have counting students for such empirical purposes. When a student transfers from a community college to a four-year college, the data systems we rely upon for statistics count those students as dropouts. Students often go to low-cost community colleges until a job opportunity arises, and re-entering the job market—with or without a certificate—is arguably the point of re-training. Despite all of this, the idea of a community college being one of the worst is antithetical to what we think and say community colleges are for. Consequently, we treat them differently than we treat for-profit colleges, even when they have similar dropout rates and poor job-placement stats. However, we treat them similarly in one vital way: we blame them both for labor market failures.

The lingo of the day to describe how we work is "the new economy." This new economy has produced a new breed of for-profit colleges that constitute a parallel education universe I have dubbed Lower Ed. More so than the mom-and-pop for-profit colleges, many of which do not even participate in federal student aid programs, these for-profit colleges—massive corporations—have added master's and doctoral degrees to their curriculums. These for-profit colleges generated billions of dollars in advertising revenue for broadcast and digital media. And these for-profit colleges were, from the start, quite clear with investors and regulators that their market niche was contingent upon deteriorating labor market conditions. Poor labor market outcomes for their graduates (and non-graduates) is part of their business plan. Regulatory penalties they might incur for having poor job-placement data is simply a cost of doing business.

This alternative argument about the expansion of for-profit colleges in the twenty-first century provides a different lens through which to view the current landscape. There is increasing federal and state interest in cracking down on for-profit colleges. Attorney David Halperin has curated a list of state, federal, and consumer protection cases filed against for-profit colleges dating back to 2009. As of early 2015, there were seventy-six cases listed. I added twelve additional cases through independent database searches to arrive at a total of eighty-eight cases. The majority of those cases, sixty-one, were launched by state agencies. Of those, the most common charge was some version of job-placement data fraud to recruit students.

Job data has become the grounds on which we not only judge the quality of for-profit colleges, but also wage regulatory battles on behalf of the public (consumer) good. Some of this emphasis is due to how we regulate for-profit colleges. The job-placement data is part of the gainful employment regulation that, to summarize, says programs that advertise as pathways to jobs must actually lead to said jobs. For-profit colleges and their main lobbying group, the Association for Private Sector Colleges and Universities, spend a lot of money pushing back on gainful employment regulations. Yet, through my interviews with for-profit college executives, I have discovered that gainful employment is treated more like an unavoidable cost of doing business than the heated political rhetoric would suggest. As one vice president of a national shareholder chain told me with a sigh, "Well, gainful employment is the cost of dealing with the Feds."

The very public fights over job-placement data and gainful employment regulations keep lots of people in business. Politicians look tough when they issue a statement in favor of gainful employment. Regulators, especially those elected to their posts, relish press releases of cases filed against predatory for-profit colleges based on job-data manipulation. For-profit colleges look like they're being led by the Department of Education to add a layer of expensive regulatory compliance against their will. They write to their investors and financial regulators about the "necessary requirements" of hiring managers of and complying with these state, federal, and consumer rules in SEC documents. Like the performance of taking our shoes off at airport security, the whole dance is a well-choreographed theater where everyone knows their parts. Like security theater, the question becomes, does it actually keep us safe? More specifically, we might wonder if the theater of regulating job-placement data and gainful employment protects the public interest amid the turmoil of the new economy. It is hard to see how it does. The premise is simple: data makes for better choices. But this assumes that better choices are available, and I'm not sure that they are.

Janice was a twenty-eight-year-old black woman enrolled in a for-profit college bachelor's program when we spoke in 2013. Her "choices" were instructive. Janice was married. Her husband "ha[d] a regular job," as she described it, meaning non-professional class. They had two children, a son who kept crashing our Skype interview because it made us laugh, and a daughter. When we met, Janice was one exam away from filing her graduation paperwork. It had taken her three years to complete because she "took off a semester when [she] ran out of money" but "by the grace of God, [they] managed a payment plan" so that she could finish on time. We talked about her career goals. She worked in a hospital. As a registered nurse, Janice was caught in the middle of a professionalization shift among nurses. Whereas the field had formerly only required a post–high school certificate in nursing, it was increasingly more common to earn a bachelor's degree in nursing.

This kind of professionalization and educational inflation falls under the "declining internal labor markets" rubric of the new economy. Unlike in the past, when experience and subsequent licensures might be obtained through an employer, in this case a hospital, the expectation now is that workers will increase their human capital at personal expense to "move up" the professional ladder. Janice's choices for promotion were limited by this context. She could hope for favorable reviews from a sympathetic management culture (a risky proposition) or she could earn a bachelor's degree in nursing. As a black woman, her path through empathetic professional cultures felt unlikely:

> All the managing nurses . . . went to the same school [a local nursing degree program] and they are nice but . . . if you want [*pause*] to be in that, well, it's not a clique but, you know how it is. All of that is, it is hard to get into and everybody respects the degree.

Janice described a workplace culture where people formed alliances with people who were similar to them. In Janice's workplace, that meant the white nurses congregated with each other at work, and sometimes socially. They had attended the same program and shared a common knowledge basis. That felt like a form of exclusion to Janice, who couldn't share in their mutual interests or history with each other.

Janice only indirectly attributed the dynamic to race, a distance that is probably similar to how that exclusion feels: ambivalent and hard to identify, but easy to feel. It could be about race only to the extent that so few black RNs had their bachelor's in nursing or had gone to the same nursing program as the nurses who had more management power. And that dynamic could be about race only to the extent that one might be less likely to have the financial means to enroll in the competitive nursing program. Because the program is one of the only ones in the local area to offer the degree, it is routinely at capacity. That means one could apply and be on a waiting list for a year or longer. Janice felt that she couldn't afford that kind of time off from greater earnings or promotability. Her ability to "afford" time could be about race and certainly about class and was likely about how all of those are always interacting at the same time.

For Janice, time and access were expensive in ways that the debt she incurred attending a for-profit degree program in nursing was not. Along the way, her husband was a huge support, except when he wasn't. "He got sensitive, I think, well, one time we had to really talk about it. Because I was like, look, I'm in it now [the program] and I know it is hard because, on everybody, my kids too. And he is real proud of me, but it was hard because I'm doing papers and he [was] working and doing the stuff here [at home]." Janice said it was hard for her husband to adjust to taking on more duties at home, in part because they were naturally her duties, as the wife and mother. He did it for the three years it took her to finish, but it put intermittent strains on their marriage. At one point, an elderly mother-like figure at Janice's church counseled her to "put [her] marriage first," meaning quit school if her husband was unhappy. Looking back on it, if Janice had known the emotional costs of going back to school, she said she might have chosen a program she could have completed faster. Those kinds of programs, the flexible ones that allow people to move through to the credential at a faster clip, are considered a for-profit college specialty.

For Mike, choice was also mostly an illusion. He could not afford the social and economic costs of dropping out of a labor market that he perceived as already stacked against him. He needed the advanced degree, but he also needed the social capital that comes with being in the workforce. London had constraints, too. She was geographically bound to an area on the losing end of economic structural change. Of the 109 students formerly or presently enrolled in a for-profit college that I interviewed over four years, 2011–2015, no one talked about the context of their college choices in ways that would suggest more accurate or clear job-placement data would have changed their circumstances or decisions.

Seventy-eight percent of them had dependent children or relatives, like aging parents. They talked about a credential as insurance against risks they could not continue to bear alone. One student, a military veteran, was particularly exasperated by the non-choices available to him. Community college was infantilizing. Traditional four-year colleges were impractical. Why should someone who has served his or her country have to "start over," was the gist of JJ's argument:

> I've led grown men in the battlefield. I've managed over 1.5 million dollars of mission-critical assets at any given time. I've taken weeks strait [*sic*] of leadership development courses. I've been directly responsible for soldiers' lives. *I needed a piece of paper that would translate my expertise to employer terms* [emphasis added].

What JJ really needed was to not need a credential at all. Like Janice and Mike, he wanted his experience and training to count. It was only when the conditions of the labor market devalued their experiences that they considered college. Job statistics won't change the conditions of the labor market for people like Janice and JJ, and there are a lot of people like Janice and JJ.

Political wrangling over job statistics looks like action, but it is mostly a distraction. Data from sociologist David Brown shows that credentials can be created without jobs to justify them, and research by Nidia Bañuelos reveals how for-profit MBA programs did not directly meet a labor market need for business graduates as much as they enrolled women and minorities who wanted a good job.[4] Also look at the case of for-profit colleges producing more massage therapists than the healthcare jobs crisis requires. A demand for good jobs does create a demand for good credentials.[5] We produce risky credentials when how we work changes dramatically, and the way we work shapes what kind of credentials we produce. If we have a shitty credentialing system, in the case of for-profit colleges, then it is likely because we have a shitty labor market. To be more precise, we have a labor market where the social contract between workers and the work on which college has previously relied has fundamentally changed and makes more workers vulnerable.

While there is a lot of academic debate about the extent of that change and whether it signals progress or decline, there is substantial evidence that suggests all of those changes shift new risks to workers.[6] Employer tenure for young workers has dropped at the same time that part-time and temporary work has increased, meaning many workers expect to change jobs more frequently, and more workers change jobs as a defined aspect of their job. Essentially, their employment is constantly temporary. As the rhetoric goes, the new economy values knowledge workers with cognitive skills, and degrees represent those kinds of skills. If that's the case, the new economy has shed high-paid but low-to-mid cognitive work in favor of high-skilled labor and low-wage, low-skilled labor. The best-case scenario proposes that this is a decade-long labor market correction. The labor market will catch back up and millions will find themselves back in "middle skill" jobs with middle-class wages and work conditions. Let's remember Mike and how the best-case scenario helps us calibrate the social cost of risk shift. In this, the best-case scenario, workers have taken on debt waiting for the market to correct itself. Depending on the kind of debt and who took it on, it's either manageable or crushing. It cannot, except in very rare instances, be discharged through bankruptcy. And for the most vulnerable workers the only way to remediate some of that debt is to accrue more of it by going back to school. If for-profit colleges like ITT are no longer around, then another form of short-term, on-demand credentials will respond to consumer demand by extracting profit from student loans and education savings accounts. That's the best-case scenario.

For students I interviewed the current scenario looks like cobbling together a career using risky credentials hoping it will make it unnecessary to ever go back to school or take on another student loan. JJ or Janice or London can be said to be negotiating the jump from low-skilled work to knowledge work. A credential is part of that jump, but so too is a set of different expectations in those respective labor markets. A host of research suggests that the culture of knowledge work is compatible with the culture of traditional college students. That is, the workers those students become will have the resources—time, money, and know-how—to put the company first and take certain "calculated" risks, like relocating or lateral career moves. Janice touched on this assumption when she said her ultimate dream was to get a doctorate in nursing because then "[her family] can stay put in this area." For researchers and politicians and financiers, credentials may represent cognitive skills and economies of the future. For the students I have talked to, a credential mostly meant insurance *against* precisely the kind of cultural assumptions that the knowledge economy wants: a worker who embraces and embodies a new type of social contract. The students I spoke with wanted the credentials so that they could keep the promised social contract of the post-industrial economy—the contract of guaranteed employment, dignified work, and health and retirement benefits. Capitalists see credentials as evidence that workers have eschewed those old-economy expectations for the new-economy realities. It is a setup for collision that dovetails with flexible, accessible credentials that can be financed when the labor market eventually and predictably sends aspirational knowledge workers back for more training.

The problem of information asymmetry, wherein prospective students are provided the information to make rational decisions about enrolling in a college, assumes that there is a rational educational choice that can be made. Given the character of the new economy, one that by definition is risky and highly variable, for millions of people that simply isn't true.

It is not an accident that financialized shareholder for-profit colleges expanded in the 2000s. Changes in how we work created demand for fast credentials. The federal student aid system made those credentials "cheap," in the sense that students do not pay much for them up front. The new economy, by all accounts, will require all of us to maintain near-constant skills training so as to be employable. The rosiest view predicts that "requiring a fundamental re-skilling mid-career, may put a greater onus on individuals or governments to extend education."[7] So far, our policy has been to rely on the student loan system to finance the onus for individuals.[8] To the extent that this has fueled for-profit colleges, our government response has positioned them as social insurance against labor market innovation (or disruption, depending on your perspective). Let me be clear: these are all conditions that are expected to sustain, if not accelerate, individual costs for job re-training repeatedly over the working life course. Our response to this has been to increase public money to private profit-extraction regimes. That is, in effect, a *negative social insurance program.* Whereas actual social insurance, like Social Security, protects workers and citizens from the vicissitudes of predatory labor market relationships, negative social insurance does not.

A negative social insurance program positions private-sector goods to profit from predictable systemic social inequalities, ostensibly for the public good. Let's return to how shareholder for-profit colleges defined their market. They said that greater inequalities in secondary schooling produced demand for higher education without a viable means for millions of people to attain it. They said that employers were less interested in providing in-house corporate training and more desiring of credentials to certify work experience. They said that the military and other public-sector employers were shedding jobs. These aren't secrets. Historically these kinds of social conditions produced public responses: public higher education expansion, childcare subsidies, and cash assistance. When systemic failures can be predicted and there exists a public response but political actors instead incentivize market solutions, a negative social insurance program results.

Social insurance like that provided through Social Security or Medicare is a pooled risk scheme. It supposes, as in the case of Social Security, that workers/citizens will age and that aging will negatively impact earnings. This produces a known outcome: greater rates of poverty. In response, a government-sponsored program used taxes or citizen payments to explicitly provide income or in-kind assistance to qualified beneficiaries. The public gets the psychic benefit of less fear about growing old and poor. Young people are able to reasonably project the kind of financial decisions they'll need to make relative to that safety net. And the public benefits when our elderly can access healthcare and afford basic needs. If the conditions of globalization and financialization and other aspects of the new economy are predictable, then we can coordinate a public response. If the new dominant work arrangement divests employers of the cost for their employees' training or certification, we can predict the effects of that. Workers will pursue certification and credentialing schemes. If we know the cost of those schemes is primarily funded through taxpayer supported federal student aid programs, then we already have a mechanism for providing social insurance. But when we facilitate spending that benefit at institutions that maximize cost to extract profit, we have perverted the public good mission of social insurance.

Early in 2016, I attended a big design conference. There were over thirty people in "education-technology" at this conference. The ed-tech providers offered everything from online platforms for massive open online courses (MOOCs) to financing schemes to help people borrow private money for a short-term coding boot camp course. All of the presentations were massive. They had professional slide shows and slick graphics. Some of these people even came with their own cordless microphones. They depicted a future of work where employers couldn't find enough "on demand," "skilled" labor for "the jobs of the future." They showed earnings gaps between those with credentials and those without. They described how inefficient graduate programs at traditional universities are because they ramp up too slowly, cost too much, and take too long to finish. One ed-tech pitch man showed a picture of a young white guy who had learned to code in two weeks. The young man had increased his earning potential by $28,000 a year. He "waltzed into" a coding job with a name-brand tech company in California. I asked for some details about the job. It was somewhat technical but we finally agreed that the job entailed basic coding for a logistics platform. I asked the ed-tech guru what would happen to the boot camp guy's skills when that project was over. Would his skills atrophy or did they apply to some other project at the company? The presenter said, of course, that he couldn't know. But, he was pleased to share information about how the boot camp was constantly adding new modules in the latest coding language for "graduates" to come back and brush up on their skills. The presenter's biggest concern was how these students would finance these programs long-term. I have different concerns. So far, we know that tech jobs are disproportionately filled with white and Asian men. We know that the tech industry has demonstrated problems hiring and promoting women and ethnic and racial minorities. We also know that access to high-tech, short-term credentials for coding and other tech-related job skills are recruiting from highly educated, high-status groups. Like the early days of for-profit college's Wall Street era, the new credentialism promises credentials in high-wage, high-demand jobs that have statistical discrimination baked into them. New institutions and new credentials are by definition lacking in prestige, the kind of prestige that lower-status workers and students need for their credential to combat discrimination in the labor market. Opening the federal student aid spigot based on the education gospel's promise without paying attention to how this ends for the poorest makes us all vulnerable. And turning on the spigot is precisely where we seem to be going.

In 2015 the Department of Education launched a pilot program to help people like those boot camp coders use federal student aid money to pay for their programs. Programs could apply for a special waiver of regulatory and statutory requirements usually associated with gaining access to federal student aid. The big one is that the program does not have to be a degree or a certificate, usually defined by some standard credit hour of attendance. And the program doesn't have to have accreditation. Without these characteristics, a boot camp or other alternative credentialing provider need not be an institution at all in any real sense. This program—the Educational Quality through Innovative Partnerships (EQUIP)—is said to encourage and reward "entrepreneurialism" in the higher education sector. The impetus for this entrepreneurial innovation? The jobs of the twenty-first century need mobile workers with specialized skills that employers will not pay for. It is the same pitch that shareholder for-profit colleges made to investors in the 1990s.

The proposed future of higher education looks a lot like the start of the Wall Street era of for-profit college expansion: occupational credentials in narrow fields, paid for through public financing schemes that start with exemplars of high-status white men in high-pay jobs and offer little hope for anyone else. By 2016 we knew how this ended for shareholder for-profit colleges but we've not yet fully counted the social cost. Mike, London, Swaggers—they show how high student loan defaults, constrained choices, predictably poor job outcomes, and negligible upward social mobility for those trapped in Lower Ed do not serve the public good. At best, Lower Ed marginally serves a few individuals, like aspirational Mikes, while trapping millions of Londons. That is barely social insurance in name only, much less the kind of social safety net all of us will need in the new economy.

EPILOGUE

For-profit colleges became a significant vehicle for the expansion of higher education in the first decade of the twenty-first century. There are two popular explanations for why that happened, and this book proposes a third. By one account, a few million people woke up in 1999 and really wanted to go to college. They wanted to go to college because their skills had atrophied or technological change had made their jobs more complex. Either way, millions of people went to college to get more, newer skills so that they could make more money. By the second account, for-profit colleges designed and executed the biggest con (on a few million people) seen in quite some time. People fell for the slick advertising, the fancy patter when they called the 1-800 number, and they didn't make the right comparisons among the best available data before choosing a college.

One account gives people far too much power while the other gives them none at all. I propose a third account, one based on three sociological concepts. The new economy produced major changes in how we work. Those changes have created more inequality, especially for women, minorities, and minority women, but not *just* for women, minorities, and minority women. Political, economic, and ideological forces, either affirmatively or by refusing to intervene, made credentials produced in the market and for the market the only feasible solution for millions of people who were made vulnerable in the new economy. This is the new credentialism. It is new because it occurs primarily in the market, profits from status-group inequalities, and offers little by way of a discernible public good.

For decades we have told stories about the American Dream that necessarily include "stay in school" and similar grand narratives. The culture meets the demand and something must respond. Our system of post–high school education has stepped up to the plate. The logic behind ever-increasing credentials is that this demand will justify all kinds of new forms of credentialing. What those forms will be is determined by the prevailing narrative of the time, shaped by the interests of powerful actors and to a lesser degree individual preferences. When demand expanded in the 1960s, the prevailing narrative was that education is a state function. Ergo, public colleges expanded. In the new economy, the prevailing narrative says that public higher education has become a cartel, or a monopoly. The solution to that, logically, is to move credentialing to the private sector where, as the John William Pope Center for Higher Education Policy said in 2016, we can do away with the "multiculturalism, collectivism, left-wing postmodernism" in public not-for-profit higher education.[1]

While both of the dominant political parties have fallen down protecting the public interest, the Republican Party is especially bullish on for-profit colleges. The Republican Party platform specifies a focus on "new systems of learning to compete with traditional four-year schools: technical institutions, online universities, life-long learning, and work-based learning in the private sector." Lower Ed thus serves multiple functions. It produces new ways of pursuing a credential that are driven by the prevailing narrative of privatization and financialization. Lower Ed focuses narrowly on training people only in skills that employers (presumably) value without also producing the above-quoted phenomena that some consider to be un-American. And it does so by primarily enrolling the students who are not accommodated by elite traditional colleges, and even some non-elite traditional colleges, because these schools cannot—or will not—change to serve them. These three forces converge, producing the horizontal and vertical stratification of higher education in the new economy: the sector continues to expand (horizontally) while also creating new levels of education (vertically). This kind of stratification might be good for a society overall, as some argue.[2] But in the United States that is true only in the aggregate and when the proportion of Lower Ed credentials is still relatively small. Political and economic power players are proposing an expansion of Lower Ed. With that comes all the evident problems of the for-profit college sector: high debt, loan defaults, regret, broken public trust, low wages, and little to no mobility from Lower Ed to Higher Ed.

In my account, for-profit colleges are something more complicated than big, evil con artists. They are an indicator of social and economic inequalities and, at the same time, are perpetuators of those inequalities. Meeting these two criteria is why for-profit colleges are Lower Ed. The growth and stability of Lower Ed is an indication that the private sector has shifted the cost of job training to workers, and the public sector has not provided a social policy response. In fact, some social policies—like the provisions in the Temporary Assistance for Needy Families legislation that required people receiving cash benefits to either be working or "enrolled in a short-term occupational educational program"— actually buoyed for-profit college enrollment. In the absence of social policy, public subsidies to Lower Ed become a negative social insurance program. A negative social insurance program is a market-based response to collective social conditions. Negative social insurance, unlike actual social insurance programs (e.g., Social Security), doesn't actually make us more secure. It only makes our collective insecurity profitable.

For-profit colleges perpetuate long-standing inequalities in gendered work, care work, racial wealth inequalities, and statistical discrimination because they grant credentials that are riskier than most traditional degrees. However, that risk is not entirely their fault. Whether or not its reasons are good or justifiable, traditional higher education has erected barriers between its institutions and for-profit colleges: transfer policies, negative bias in admissions, and hiring practices. While those barriers may serve to protect the students earning traditional college credentials, they trap those with for-profit college credits or credentials in an educational ghetto.

Even as for-profit college enrollment returns to pre–boom cycle enrollment numbers, they are still the market (and public) solution to constantly retraining America's workforce for "the jobs of the twenty-first century" that people, including President Barack Obama, tout. In the wake of the very public woes faced by for-profit colleges, other market-based credentials are vying for a slice of the credential profit pie. Coding boot camps, once an oddity created by the peculiar labor conditions of Silicon Valley, are spreading. As they spread, their tuition prices increase and angel investors look for ways to financialize that tuition. Today, two boot-camp financing companies are offering private student loans so that workers can pay up to $18,000 for courses that last from one day to a few weeks. The Department of Education issued a special grant program so that traditional colleges can offer similar programs and students can use federal student aid money to pay for them. The quest has become cheaper—better labor at little to no cost for employers. That is unsustainable. Developing people takes time and money, two things that the new economy stresses to the breaking point.

So what's the solution? I admit, sociologists aren't very good at solutions. The obvious response is that the large scale of the problem makes it one that only a large-scale social policy can address. This is not a problem for a technological innovation or a market product. This requires politics. Politics that, especially in our current political climate, will need social movements to prod real change along. Given the interconnections between the wealth inequalities that make workers susceptible to student loan debt, the prestige hierarchy that makes student loan debt the only way millions can get any credential, and the labor market discrimination that makes it all far too risky, the social movements must be multi-pronged. They would address the root cause of declining union power to effectively procure better social contract conditions for all workers and not just those elite workers in Silicon Valley. Those social movements would also address, head-on, the racist and gendered histories of wealth inequalities in the United States and their impact on minorities in the new economy. Wealth buffers income spikiness and insecurity. If the latter is projected to increase for more workers it will necessarily come first and stay the longest for those with the least wealth. In the United States that is about our history of enslavement, apartheid, and the New Jim Crow of the carceral continuum from school to prison. And, social movements would have to address the limits of private-sector employment to provide the social and economic security that is a basic human right.

There is hope.

In 2013, George Zimmerman was found not guilty of killing seventeen-year-old Trayvon Martin as Trayvon walked home from a neighborhood store in the neighborhood where he and Zimmerman lived. For many young people, this was their first taste of radical injustice. Many also mark it as the beginning of what would become known as Black Lives Matter (BLM). By all accounts, BLM is a decentralized social justice movement. It is certainly national. One can argue that it is even global, with recent spread of BLM slogans to Brazil and France, for example. BLM's central platform is anti–police brutality, which makes it seem, at first blush, a strange entrant into our conversation about labor markets and credentials and negative social insurance. But in 2016, BLM continued a long tradition of social movements that have articulated policy positions that address the root causes of the issue on which the movement was founded. In this policy platform we see seeds of hope for articulating and organizing a social movement response to negative social insurance schemes.

For all the media coverage that BLM has attracted, its policy platform received markedly less coverage. That is a shame because it is a remarkable document. Officially released by the "Movement for Black Lives," the document represents policy issues from over fifty BLM-affiliated organizations. They call it "A Vision for Black Lives" and it is a vision that could improve the lives of everyone. The platform has six broad categories. Two of them are directly applicable: economic justice and reparations. In reparations, the plan calls out the historical connections so evident in London's path to her for-profit college. The "cradle-to-college" pipeline, as they call it, is broken for millions of Americans and it is most broken for poor blacks and minorities. The plan rightfully points out something that should be clear in this book:

> The rising costs of higher education and exploitative and predatory lending practices of private and for-profit institutions make Black students more likely to drop-out, and leave them and their families stuck with debilitating and crippling debt. U.S. student loan debt nearly totals $1.3 trillion, with close to $900 billion in federal student loans, and more than 7 million borrowers in default.

The platform rightfully alludes not only to the expansion of risky credentials but to the financialization—or predatory—lending and financing schemes that make them so profitable for speculators. The default statistic suggests that this is a systemic problem, produced by wealth inequalities, justified by contemporary income inequalities and perpetuated by corporate-political interests.

The platform also addresses the need for economic justice, namely a living wage and public subsidies to improve the quality of low-wage jobs. Both of these issues are about the relative nature of debt that is so clear in the Swaggers' experience of it. These issues also address the constrained choices that make risky credentials attractive and profitable. On many levels, the BLM policy platform addresses the root causes of how and why risky credentials are a systemic social failure. It also provides ways forward that make sense.

Similarly, Strike Debt is one of the most significant social movements to come out of the public discourse on student loan debt.[3] In 2014, an advocacy group, The Rolling Jubilee, bought thousands of dollars of for-profit college student loan debt for pennies on the dollar. Because of the securitization discussed in Chapter 1, debt can be bought on secondary markets. Usually debt collectors buy it for cheap and hope to harass debtors into repaying it at a profit. The Rolling Jubilee bought the debt . . . and forgave it. Since then, the fifteen former Corinthian College students who were released from their suffocating financial burden started the Corinthian 15 (now the Corinthian 100) to lobby for loan forgiveness. Strike Debt, The Rolling Jubilee, and dozens of other groups were instrumental to putting debt, one important symbol of the risk shift, in the national spotlight.

Economists and public policy professors Darrick Hamilton and William "Sandy" Darity Jr. say that if for-profit colleges are about demand, then let's reduce demand.[4] In 2009, DeVry University president David Pauldine said, "I have heard repeatedly from our admissions offices that when they interview prospective students, they're saying they just lost their job or fear that they might lose their job."[5] If job insecurity creates demand, one way to alleviate that is to address job insecurity. Here, too, social movements help. The Fight for 15 organizers have fought and won minimum wage increases. The Fight for 15 represents mostly minority, female service and care workers. Basically, women who would be likely for-profit college students—and are currently working in the fastest-growing jobs in this polarized labor market—organized to improve the quality of bad jobs. Their fight shows that job quality can be improved without funneling millions of people into for-profit credentialing programs. Hamilton and Darity also suggest that a federal jobs program could alleviate demand for risky credentials by putting a floor beneath the labor market. Whether we are experiencing a temporary lag as the labor market restructures or a permanent change into a bifurcated job market, providing some social insurance for millions of people would remove the profit from job insecurity. These are all more fiscally and morally responsible than encouraging everyone to go to college by any means necessary.

Student loan debt remediation following the Great Recession and rapid expansion of the negative social insurance scheme of for-profit credentialing might warrant a special policy solution. At any rate, a once-in-a-lifetime debt bubble deserves public policy attention. Calls for free or near-free tuition at public colleges are an important part of a solution. But they don't address the twenty-five years when policy encouraged for-profit credential expansion. All higher education policy too rarely engages the inefficiencies in labor markets as job guarantee programs would do. There are robust arguments about the extent to which federal jobs programs are regressive. But they are hypothetical. In contrast, we know for a fact that education savings programs, tax deductions for student loan interest rates, and stratified higher education financing schemes are regressive. In the case of for-profit colleges, the poorest citizens paid the most relative to their wealth, income, and labor market returns for credentials and they are less likely to earn the tax code benefits to offset them. By any stretch of the imagination, credentialing in the new economy has to date taken from the have-nots to give to the haves.

On a final personal note, I am a black woman. I would be remiss if I didn't speak directly to whether or not the ways that for-profit colleges operate are gendered or racist. I spent a year traveling to for-profit colleges while writing my dissertation. I talked to over forty people at for-profit colleges during that time. People ask me all the time how I tricked them into talking to me. I didn't have to "trick" anyone. In none of my visits did anyone ever ask me about my educational background. If they had, I was prepared to tell the truth. At the time, I had a bachelor's degree but not yet a doctorate. I would have said, "I have a bachelor's degree." But no one asked. As a black woman, I fit the likely student profile. They assumed I had children, no husband, no significant educational background, and very little knowledge about college. I doubt that a white woman or a man would have gotten the same data that I was able to get, because the process is actually designed to enroll someone like me. Is that gendered or racist? It depends on what you think those words mean.

We live in an age of colorblind delusions, so it is possible to think that intent makes something sexist or racist. I'm a sociologist. For me, perpetuating the inequalities resulting from inter-generational cumulative disadvantage doesn't require intent. In fact, racism and sexism work best of all when intent is not a prerequisite. By this measure, when for-profit colleges design a speedy enrollment process because women have so little flexible time, or assume that I need a job to support my kids, they are profiting from inequality. No intent required.

ACKNOWLEDGMENTS

I signed my very first book contract ever with The New Press when I was a fourth-year PhD student at Emory University. Bless the entirety of Tara Grove's heart, but she thought that I could pull it off. As my editor, Tara has been patient and sharp and kind. I had one caveat when she asked if I might be interested in writing a book. "I won't do sensationalism," I said. She agreed, and not once has she deviated. Tara also pushed me to use own my voice. "This is *your* book," she said, long before I could fathom that was possible. I owe her a great deal. Similarly, Ken Wissoker of Duke University Press took a call from a nobody, anxious about her first real smart person project. He explained the business of publishing and gave me clear-eyed advice. He also encouraged me to sign that "very, very good deal with a very, very good press" without adding, "you idiot!" I really appreciate that. Jeffrey Alan Johnson, Louise Seamster, Matt Reed, and Anne Kress provided critical reads of early drafts.

I also owe my mentors a huge dose of gratitude. Richard Rubinson never blinked an eye as I took on these huge tasks. It is almost as if he trusted that I could pull it off. He taught me almost everything I know about political economies, credentialism, and research design. Sandy Darity and Darrick Hamilton are the kinds of economists that we need more of. Their work in stratification economics influences a lot of my thinking on possible social policies to disrupt the cycle of credential inflation and inequality. Gaye Tuchman has always championed my intellectual aspirations, and I owe her for that. She has been my co-author, unflinchingly honest reader, and great friend. Myra Marx Ferree cited this book while it was still early in pre-press. That's a huge vote of confidence to a junior scholar, and I thank her. Barbara Ehrenreich doesn't know me from a hole in the wall, but her work has inspired my approach to communicating the context of academic research for many years. Stephanie Coontz has also influenced my approach to this work, and she was so kind to me at a national sociology conference. She was also fierce, telling me, "Don't do that thing where you apologize for yourself!" Kind but fierce is kind of my favorite thing. Stephanie has that in spades.

Cathy Davidson reached out to me and offered to review early copies of the book. I couldn't believe it then, and I still can't. Carol Anderson read my dissertation, told me I was a "bad, bad girl," and gave me the go-ahead to explore this really big story that I thought I could tell. Dorothy Brown staged several interventions when my confidence wavered, always insisting that the mirror she held up to me was the accurate one despite my protestations that I needed a smaller, cracked mirror. Every time I mumbled to myself, "You can do this," I was channeling Dorothy.

My colleagues allowed me the room to work on this project during my first year as a tenure-track professor. That is unheard of. Their generosity belies stories about cutthroat, selfish academics. I would also like to thank Bisma Rais and Olivia Pryor for their research assistance.

Bless each of my dear friends who read early drafts, gave me space as I wrestled with ideas, and trusted me to finally get here—the finish line. I love you Vivian, Jade, Patricia, Phil, Ashley, and Melissa. And to all who fed me, loved me, and poured drinks (alcoholic and not) into me while I persevered, thank you. Finally, it wouldn't be any work of mine if I didn't thank Gabrielle. Always.

METHODOLOGICAL NOTES

As discussed in the introduction, some of the framing of this book includes my personal narrative. Sociologists call this an autoethnographic approach. Other parts of this book include primary data collected during the course of a case study. What follows outlines a discussion of those methods, by chapter. Additional resources, including an interactive bibliography on for-profit higher education and credentialism, can be found at www.tressiemc.com/lowered.

Introduction

In 2014, I extracted all of the Securities and Exchange Commission filings. Data are from the SEC prospectuses filed by every for-profit college between 1995 and 2009. 1995 coincides with the Wall Street era's period of 1994 to present. The data are a census of all such filings listed by the SEC with the unique industry-sector code "Educational-Services." The list includes eighteen prospectuses. To organize the data, I treated each prospectus as a case.

I began the analysis by assigning a set of categorical variables to each case. Variables included name, location, date, financial holdings, enrollment, and other descriptors. These data were entered into a mixed-methods analysis software program (Dedoose). Working from sociological theory and literature on other types of credentialing, as well as the specific instance of for-profit college credentials, I created a coding scheme to analyze the data. The coding scheme included themes related to labor markets, occupations, recruitment processes, accreditation, professional organizations, and organizational structure.

Working from the coding scheme, I analyzed the frequency of patterns across and within cases, by various combinations of the categorical variables. A full treatment of the findings falls outside the scope of this book, but it included a systematic textual analysis method common in critical discourse analysis.

3. Jesus Is My Backup Plan

Between September 2012 and December 2013, I interviewed ninety-six students currently enrolled in a shareholder college (those included in the analysis from the Introduction). This represented nine schools at thirteen locations in Atlanta, Georgia. I used a combination of recruitment and sampling methods to construct a sample of twenty-two men and seventy-four women, ages twenty-four to forty-five. Respondents were recruited online and in person at school sites. I used referral (or "snowball sampling") techniques to recruit additional participants.

Using a semi-structured interview guide, I interviewed students at least once, although some relationships included multiple interviews during the course of the study. The interview guide had four themes: motivations, experiences, aspirations, and narratives of legitimacy. Essentially, I wanted to explore how students came to choose a for-profit college, the broader social context of that choice, how they experienced their for-profit college, how they planned to use their credential, and if they thought they attended a "real college."

Interviews were mostly recorded (save three, due to technical difficulties or maximizing an unexpected interview opportunity).

When I didn't have a recording, I used standard fieldwork note-taking practices to record our interactions. Transcripts and field notes were analyzed using Dedoose. I did three waves of coding, using a coding scheme and open-ended coding for emergent themes.

4. When Higher Education Makes Cents

In 2013, I participated in the enrollment process at nine for-profit colleges in the greater Atlanta, Georgia, area. Each site was a shareholder for-profit college brand. I did limit my sample to those with physical campuses. For each site, I called or filled out an online form to initiate contact. I took the standard enrollment campus tour at each field site. I also collected marketing materials. I used all of my own personal information during the process. I did not complete the financial aid process (which would constitute fraud). I observed the process from first contact through the first opportunity to sign an enrollment agreement.

I also tracked the number, frequency, and content of follow-up phone calls and messages from the for-profit colleges. I was interested in how the pain-funnel technique worked for a non-responsive prospective student. I was also interested in whether those techniques differed by the type of for-profit college. Did "higher status" for-profit colleges, like those that only offered graduate programs in the wealthier part of town, pursue prospects in the same way as the "lower status" for-profit colleges with offices at the local mall did?

Field notes, marketing materials, and transcripts of calls were coded and systematically analyzed. Two open-ended coding waves produced themes that I triangulated with additional sources (e.g., Senate HELP reports, consumer agency violation claims, and media accounts).

My study of a group of online for-profit college students, the

Swaggers, was conducted over nine months in 2014. I interviewed twenty-one members. I followed standard social media research protocols regarding privacy and ethics. I advertised my position as a researcher to the group on twenty-nine occasions by making posts to the group's wall. I spoke with the group's moderator twice for permission to post and engage. I issued standard institutional review board documentation to respondents recruited from the group. Data on the age and racial makeup of the group is from a survey that the group's moderator made available to me.

I used a digital research method that included a content analysis of respondents' posts and interviews with those respondents. The interviews were all conducted using Skype. I used the respondents' Facebook posts as a narrative journal to prime their memories of what led them to post. This method has been shown to increase recall and greater reflection. My semi-structured interview guide was modeled on the one described in Chapter 3. Transcripts were coded and analyzed.

NOTES

Introduction: The Education Gospel

1. David J. Deming, Claudia Goldin, and Lawrence F. Katz, "The For-Profit Postsecondary School Sector: Nimble Critters or Agile Predators?" *Journal of Economic Perspectives* 26, no. 1 (2013): 139–64.

2. You can even take horribly named "are you smarter than a football player?" Wonderlic tests online. See more on Wonderlic use at for-profit colleges: Frank Donoghue, "For-Profits' Dubious Use of Entrance Exams," *The Chronicle of Higher Education* (April 18, 2011).

3. I talk about the difference between counseling and closing in Chapter 5. The gist of it is that we often discuss these as if they are the same thing. That is because the activities are the same. Counselors (or "enrollment agents/representatives") at elite traditional schools, community colleges, small liberal arts colleges, and for-profit colleges perform fairly similar tasks. Thanks to a cottage industry called enrollment management, which uses accountability and predictive analytics tools to meet institution enrollment goals, traditional and for-profit colleges increasingly borrow heavily from each other because they use the same software to manage their revenue-generating enrollment process. They identify the ideal likely student, they establish some kind of rapport with that ideal student, they encourage enrollment, and they meet enrollment goals or targets. Why is this "closing" when for-profits do it? For one, the ways in which many for-profit colleges establish rapport and meet enrollment targets can be far more aggressive than most traditional colleges would allow: frequent contact, sharing "leads" for years, using behavioral selling techniques that draw on students' fears to motivate them, etc. Some researchers call this intrusive counseling a benefit for students who don't know how to "do" college in the traditional way (for example: Regina Deil Amen and James Rosenbaum's 2003 study, "The Social Pre-Requisites of Success: Can College Structure Reduce the Need for Social Know-How?"). But researchers Bonnie Fox Garrity, Mark Garrison, and Roger Fiedler put it nicely when they asked, "access to what,"

exactly? As in, this kind of closing makes it easier for students without the social know-how to do college to then do *what*? Closing a prospective student is different for the ends of the enrollment than it is for the means of enrollment. For-profit colleges, especially shareholder for-profit colleges, close students to manage operating budgets and profit projections. That is closing no matter what the activities are.

4. Despite public perception, for-profit colleges did not and do not only draw older students. Many, like the technical college where I worked, had dedicated staff to conduct high school college fairs, in-home family recruitment visits, and other activities aimed at students fresh from high school. The documents that publicly traded for-profit colleges file with the Securities and Exchange Commission frequently list high school recruitment as a key marketing strategy. Some schools, like the Art Institutes' parent company at the time of filing in 2001, dedicated as many as a quarter of their enrollment staff to recruiting these students. Traditional-aged students were often considered more valuable for the prestige they might lend the school ("a real college has traditional students"), but the leadership on the ground at for-profit colleges also saw these students as difficult to close because they often brought family members with them. Parents and family ask different questions and present roadblocks to closing. For example, completing these students' federal financial aid paperwork typically requires a parent's tax information. This meant more stakeholders, which could undermine the greatest commodity at the for-profit college: time. Working with the high school students was a slightly more prestigious role, even if the conversions were harder won.

5. This process of priming motivations to close sales and get students to that critical first day of class is common at for-profit colleges. A 2012 Senate investigation of for-profit colleges cites one school's name for it: the pain funnel. Both the practice and the term aren't unique to for-profit colleges. It's a common sales technique. I discuss how and why this works in the for-profit college context in Chapter 4.

6. These short-term loans became a serious issue for some for-profit colleges a decade later when regulatory oversight increased and the financial bubble began to deflate. One such program, PEAKS, created in 2010 (around the time that I was in a meeting with that executive), sold securities to investors to raise cash that it then lent to students. As one might imagine, the loans were high interest. Students did not have a choice of lenders as they do with federal student loans. This generally means a captive market with little bargaining power. If this sounds similar to the housing finance schemes that precipitated the Great Recession, there is good

reason. Like the millions of dollars in bad mortgages that were issued, many using similar securities structures, these loans had very high default rates. The issuing for-profit college (ITT Technical Institute) had guaranteed these loans. The Securities and Exchange Commission charged in 2014 that ITT Technical Institute misled investors about the risk of those loans and then tried to obscure the impact of the loan defaults in financial statements. This included creative accounting and even making short-term loan payments to keep students current through filing periods.

7. ITT Technical Institute stopped enrolling students and went out of business in September 2016 at the time of this writing.

8. The 90-10 Rule is a federal law that bars for-profit colleges from generating more than 90 percent of their revenue from federal student aid programs, including loans and grants. Most traditional colleges generate non-tuition revenue from things like sports programs, research, patents, and real estate—all things for-profit colleges do not have or do (save a few exceptions; e.g., two for-profit colleges have sports teams). One way to think about the 90-10 Rule is that any number you hear that a for-profit college generated is almost entirely extracted from tax-supported federal financial aid programs and then distributed to owners.

9. Education Management Corporation, 1999. Archived with the Securities and Exchange Commission. Retrieved from https://www.sec.gov/Archives/edgar/data/880059/0000950128-96-000569.txt January 18, 2014.

10. Strayer College Prospectus, 1996. Archived with the Securities and Exchange Commission. Retrieved from https://www.sec.gov/Archives/edgar/data/1013934/0000950133-96-001268.txt January 18, 2014.

11. ITT Technical Institute Prospectus, 1998. Archived with the Securities and Exchange Commission. Retrieved from https://www.sec.gov/Archives/edgar/data/922475/0000950124-98-003234.txt January 18, 2014.

12. Corinthian Colleges Prospectus, 1999. Archived with the Securities and Exchange Commission. Retrieved from https://www.sec.gov/Archives/edgar/data/1066134/0001017062-99-000150.txt January 18, 2014.

13. From "The Economics of Higher Education: A Report Prepared by the Department of Treasury with the Department of Education," issued December 2012. Available at Education Resources Information Center: https://archive.org/details/ERIC_ED544780.

14. For sure, federal Pell grant and other aid programs did expand during this era, mostly to account for declining state investments. But the expansions could not be considered massive. Neither were they particularly brave given the size of the

issue and the backdrop of the Great Recession. The contentious political climate is partially to blame, but so too is a turn away from massive Great Society–type programs in favor of market-based solutions.

15. Later, I would ask this question empirically: do for-profit colleges hire their own graduates? That's a critical question if the issue is whether a college is real, i.e., legitimate, or not. One of the ways a new type of institution, like for-profit colleges, can become more legitimate is to behave more like real colleges (often called isomorphism). And one of the ways that real colleges became real and have maintained that legitimacy is by creating a labor market for their own graduates. To work in a college, even in low-level administrative support work, one generally needs to have a college degree from an accredited institution. When I surveyed job ads listed by for-profit colleges in higher education newspapers in 2013, I found that only two ads of eighty-nine mentioned a college degree as a requirement, much less one from a similar institution. But that doesn't say that for-profit colleges don't hire their own. It only says that it doesn't hire like real colleges. Another survey of the educational backgrounds of the executive boards and academic leadership of for-profit colleges, also done in 2013, found only one school executive—then president Craig D. Swenson of for-profit Argosy University—had both an advanced degree (a PhD) and a degree from a for-profit college (Walden University).

16. "Sleepy sector" is perhaps the most cliché phrase in all of the writing on for-profit colleges. The phrase can be attributed to easily half a dozen books and many more articles. For the sake of rigor, I will say that is from a 2012 *Chronicle of Higher Education* article by Kim Strosnider: "For-Profit Higher Education Sees Booming Enrollments and Revenues" in *The Chronicle of Higher Education* 44, no. 20 (January 23, 1998).

17. For example, I discuss connections between the Clinton Foundation and for-profit college behemoth Laureate Education in "The Great Ambivalence" in *False Choices: The Faux Feminism of Hillary Rodham Clinton*, ed. Liza Featherstone (New York: Verso Books, 2016), 118.

18. The theory of skillification argues that there is a "skills gap" between the skills American workers have, the skills employers in the new economy will pay for, and the knowledge the economy needs. Much of the debate about the extent to which there is an actual skills gap in the labor market can be read in Autor versus Kalleberg. David Autor, "The Polarization of Job Opportunities in the US Labor Market: Implications for Employment and Earnings," Center for American Progress and the Hamilton Project (2010). Arne L. Kalleberg, "Good Jobs, Bad

Jobs." New York: Russell Sage Foundation (2012). These are primarily debates about the extent to which ours is a down period of cyclical economic job growth or to which technological change has decimated middle-skills jobs, respectively. I tend to fall in line with Kalleberg but neither argues that a skills gap exists the way popular discourse (especially among politicians) frames it. Instead, the empirical debate is about the extent to which there is structural change in the labor market. Essentially, even those at odds agree that at the moment, many workers are experiencing low wages and poor economic prospects. The only real argument is whether that change is permanent or a natural correction as labor markets change.

19. Researcher Charlie Eaton argues, quite convincingly, that the diffusion of shareholder ideologies through the for-profit college sector led to organizational transformations most notable in the sector's aggressive enrollment strategies. See: Charlie Eaton, "Shareholder Value, Ownership Form, and the Transformation of US For-Profit Colleges Since 1997," in 28th Annual Meeting, Society for the Advancement of Socio-Economics, Berkeley, California (2016).

20. U.S. Government Accountability Office, "For-Profit Colleges: Undercover Testing Finds Colleges Encouraged Fraud and Engaged in Deceptive and Questionable Marketing Practices," Report GAO-10-948T, August 4, 2010. Available at http://www.gao.gov/products/GAO-10-948T, accessed August 18, 2012.

21. This is a standard social science finding that can sound controversial when said in public discourse. To qualify: higher education admits students and groups of students based on many indicators that map onto class, race, and gender. Even if the eventual degree or credential earned leads to social mobility or well-being, we say that higher education benefits from a certain degree and type of inequality. This is such a truism in my field that I struggle to name a single good reference for it. For a recent treatment, one could see Ann L. Mullen, *Degrees of Inequality: Culture, Class, and Gender in American Higher Education* (Baltimore: Johns Hopkins University Press, 2010), or almost any other citation in this book.

1. The Real

1. One of the best resources on higher education accreditation is Paul Gaston, *Higher Education Accreditation: How It's Changing, Why It Must* (Sterling, VA: Stylus Publishing, 2013). I cannot argue with the history outlined in the book, although I admit to being less bullish about changing accreditation until there is a sense of what we are changing it to do. There is a slightly longer conversation about

accreditation in later chapters, but a fuller discussion is outside the scope of this book. Still, it's worth noting that accreditation isn't the policing body the public often thinks that it is. Also, accreditation agencies are stratified, serving different types of institutions. They are also member-based organizations, meaning they rely on dues paid by member institutions. I agree with the many people who argue that this creates a disincentive to sanction institutions that behave badly. However, without a nationwide definition of "quality," making accreditation more efficient solves a symptom rather than the disease.

2.   Economists love this question. The most cited research in this area is from Stephanie Riegg Cellini and Latika Chaudhary, "The Labor Market Returns to a For-Profit College Education," *Economics of Education Review* 43 (2014): 125–40. They show that for-profit associate's degree holders have a small positive return to their credential but conclude that given how much more expensive for-profits are than community colleges, the debt outstrips these modest gains. Kevin Lang and Russell Weinstein argue that they have better data (it's literally in the paper's title: "The Wage Effects of Not-for-Profit and For-Profit Certifications: Better Data, Somewhat Different Results," *Labour Economics* 14 [2013]: 230–43.) They find that "most certificates from for-profit and non-profit institutions don't raise earnings."

3.   For those who like to get in the weeds, Cellini and Goldin also find that this is true across different types of for-profit colleges. This means there isn't much of a prestige hierarchy among for-profit colleges; i.e., going to Strayer is like going to Everest is like going to the University of Phoenix. One of my favorite ways to explain this is from field experiments where researchers send resumes to employers. These resumes list either for-profit colleges or traditional colleges. One study by Rajeev Darolia, Cory Koedel, Paco Martorell, Katie Wilson, and Francisco Perez-Arce finds that employers do not show a preference for resumes that list a for-profit credential, even over resumes that list no credential at all ("Do Employers Prefer Workers Who Attend For-Profit Colleges? Evidence from a Field Experiment," *Journal of Policy Analysis and Management* 34, no. 4 [2015]: 881–903). Researchers Nicole Deterding and David Pedulla give a plausible reason for this: employers don't have the mechanisms to determine whether a credential is for-profit or not ("Educational Authority in the 'Open Door' Marketplace: Labor Market Consequences of For-Profit, Non-Profit, and Fictional Credentials," *Sociology of Education* 89, no. 3 [2016]: 155–70). Like Darolia and colleagues, Deterding and Pedulla sent out resumes with different types of degree listed. For-profit college

degrees didn't fare better than degrees from fictional colleges. The take-away could be that degrees without recognizable names don't fare well *and* if an employer can discern that a credential is from a for-profit college it really isn't better than having no credential at all. And none of this addresses the reality for the majority of those who enroll in a for-profit college, who will leave *without* any credential.

4. "Are Career Colleges Credible?," *News & Notes*, National Public Radio, air date March 13, 2007. Available at http://www.npr.org/templates/story/story.php ?storyId=7870930.

5. Anna Chung, "For-Profit Student Heterogeneity," *Economics of Education Review* 31, no. 6 (2008): 1084–101. doi:10.1016/j.econedurev.2012.07.004.

6. One notable exception: William Beaver, "For-Profit Higher Education: A Social and Historical Analysis," *Sociological Viewpoints* 25 (2009): 53.

7. Jonathan Guryan and Matthew Thompson, "Report on Gainful Employment," Charles River Associates, April 2, 2010.

8. Mary Nguyen, "Degreeless in Debt: What Happens to Borrowers Who Drop Out," *Education Sector*, 2012. Retrieved from http://eric.ed.gov/?id=ED529 758 August 1, 2014. Also see Adam Looney and Constantine Yannelis, "A Crisis in Student Loans? How Changes in the Characteristics of Borrowers and in the Institutions They Attended Contributed to Rising Loan Defaults," Brookings Papers on Economic Activity Conference paper series, September 10–11, 2015. Washington, D.C.

9. Sociologists David K. Brown and David B. Bills acknowledge that there is a "lacuna of ethnographic research on credentialing processes that could be vastly expanded to yield valuable insights" (2011, 135) in their article on the sociology of credentials. I hope this book is a small step in that direction. David K. Brown and David B. Bills, "An Overture for the Sociology of Credentialing: Empirical, Theoretical, and Moral Considerations," *Research in Social Stratification and Mobility* 29, no. 1 (2011): 133–8.

10. Guilbert C. Hentschke, Vicente M. Lechuga, and William G. Tierney, *For-Profit Colleges and Universities: Their Markets, Regulation, Performance, and Place in Higher Education* (Herndon, VA: Stylus Publishing, 2010).

11. U.S. Department of Education, National Center for Education Statistics [NCES], 2011; U.S. Government Accountability Office [GAO], 2010.

12. See: Diverse Issues in Higher Education annual top producers of black degree holders, updated annually at http://diverseeducation.com/top100.

13. Ibid.

14. This framework for understanding for-profit colleges is one I share with other researchers, including David K. Brown and David B. Bills. It is also the least common approach in the work that has been published by academic journals.

15. I borrow most of this framing of the Wall Street era from Kevin Kinser's excellent institutional history of the for-profit college sector (Kevin Kinser, *From Main Street to Wall Street: The Transformation of For-Profit Higher Education* [San Francisco: Jossey-Bass, 2006]). There are other texts about the sector, but many veer too much toward boosterism to provide much in the way of a framework for understanding for-profit college's trajectory. Kinser's book stands out for doing that.

16. Goldie Blumenstyk, *American Higher Education in Crisis? What Everyone Needs to Know* (New York: Oxford University Press, 2014).

17. Ibid.

18. Capella Education, 2006. Archived with the Securities and Exchange Commission at https://www.sec.gov/Archives/edgar/data/1104349/0000950137 06012322/c07996b1e424b1.htm.

19. NCES, 2005, 2006, in Hentschke et al. 2010: 3.

20. The professional holdout in the for-profit college encroachment is medical schools. This might sound odd when one considers how many health fields for-profit colleges specialize in. But certifying nursing assistants is a different business from producing medical doctors. The latter has a very strong lobby in the American Medical Association and stiff competition for the prestige of producing medical doctors. There are a few exceptions, all of them in lower-status subfields of the medical field: osteopathic medicine (Rocky Vista University College in Parker, Colorado) and chiropractic schools. This does suggest that what sociologists call professional enclosure—quite literally the control or enclosure of access to a profession—can have a significant impact on the growth of for-profit colleges.

21. Gregory Gilpin, Joe Saunders, and Christina Stoddard, "Why Have For-Profit Colleges Expanded So Rapidly? The Role of Labor Market Changes in Student Enrollment and Degree Completion at Two-Year Colleges," *Economics of Education Review* 45 (2015): 53–63.

22. Julie Margetta Morgan and Ellen-Marie Whelan, "Profiting from Health Care: The Role of For-Profit Schools in Training the Health Care Workforce," report for Center for American Progress, January 2011.

23. Ibid.

24. It is important to note that the sector remains diverse, comprised of small schools as well as large shareholder organizations.

25. Randy Martin, *Financialization of Daily Life* (Philadelphia: Temple University Press, 2002).

26. Eileen Appelbaum, Annette Bernhardt, and Richard J. Murnane, eds., *Low-Wage America: How Employers Are Reshaping Opportunity in the Workplace* (New York: Russell Sage Foundation, 2003). Arne Kalleberg, *Good Jobs, Bad Jobs: The Rise of Polarized and Precarious Employment Systems in the United States, 1970s to 2000s* (New York: Russell Sage Foundation, 2011).

27. I argue in my research that the best way to understand for-profit colleges is as gendered organizations. Women out-pace men in enrollment at all levels of education, but women's dominance at for-profits is high even by those standards. In the aggregate, almost 75 percent of for-profit college students are women. Some campuses I toured for research reported 100 percent female enrollment. During my time at the Beauty College, I only ever enrolled two men. I enrolled more at the Technical College. Further, the programs that make up the bulk of for-profit colleges' market share certify workers in fields that are considered gendered: allied health (see: Celia Davies, "The Sociology of Professions and the Profession of Gender," *Sociology* 30, no.4 [1996]: 661–78 for an overview as well as recent research by Adia Harvey Wingfield and Christine L. Williams); education (Christine L. Williams's edited volume, *Doing "Women's Work"* [Christine L. Williams, ed., *Doing "Women's Work": Men in Nontraditional Occupations* Vol. 3. Sage Publications, 1993] is a good primer on this); and office assistance. Allied health is especially gendered in light of the low-status roles they certify and the gender-based pay discrepancies in the jobs that fall in this category. Essentially, for-profit colleges use a gendered model of enrollment (intrusive or "other mothering") to disproportionately enroll women in fields that are disproportionately dominated by women already: largely care fields associated with "female traits" and accompanied with the low status and pay associated with "women's work."

28. Time has become a scarce and contested commodity in the new economy. Sociologist Arlie Russell Hochschild talked about the "time bind" in her famous book *The Time Bind: When Work Becomes Home and Home Becomes Work* (New York: Henry Holt, 1997). Briefly, the argument is that as the Western middle-class standard of living has afforded us more "stuff," globalization means working more to afford it. The stuff becomes a stand-in for the time we devote to accruing it. Before she was a political star, Elizabeth Warren wrote a book with Amelia Tyagi called *The Two-Income Trap: Why Middle-Class Mothers and Fathers Are Going Broke* (New York: Basic Books, 2007). Much like Hochschild, they argued that the

conditions of middle-class work made families vulnerable. Stagnant wages and rising housing, healthcare, and education costs made a two-income family a necessity. But the cost of replacing all the labor done in the home made working outside of it a risky financial bet. Yet even all of this, of course, assumes that this is a new phenomenon for middle-class families. As research has shown, this has long been the reality for African American families, poor families, and working-class families. In large part, these families have only ever known a time bind, trapped by the allure of a two-income normative family structure. Essentially, the new economy has made more middle-class people feel poor and working class.

29. I talk more about the transferability of for-profit college credits in a later chapter. There is also qualitative evidence that traditional graduate school programs have a negative bias against applicants' for-profit college credentials and in hiring (Jonathan Adams and Margaret H. DeFleur, "The Acceptability of a Doctoral Degree Earned Online As a Credential for Obtaining a Faculty Position," *The American Journal of Distance Education* 19, no. 2 [2005]: 71–85).

30. The prevailing policy and research narrative is that we will all need to become "lifelong learners." Currently, over half of all those enrolled in post-secondary education that qualifies to issue federal student aid uses said aid. How will people pay for higher education forever? One solution is to make higher education cheaper. That is the aim of efforts like massive open online courses (MOOCs) and similar models of on-demand free or cheap education. Jason Reich, now of MIT, is one of the best researchers on the design, utility, and efficacy of these programs (see Jason Reich, "Thoughts on Digital Equity at Harvard Graduate School of Education," November 14, 2011, at Harvard Graduate School of Education, Boston, MA. Retrieved from http://www.gse.harvard.edu/news/11/11/thoughts-digital-equity -justin-reich). He has found that students in these programs are generally better educated, with more social and economic resources, than the kinds of people most vulnerable in a labor market that increasingly requires a post-secondary education. Yet, there is scant evidence that employers value these non-degree programs or similar certificate programs, like badges. Coding boot camps are the latest iteration of this approach. These promise certifications in high-demand, high-paying "good jobs" like software coding. But some of these programs are actually quite expensive (the highest-cost boot camp I have recorded charges $18,000). The evidence is both preliminary and mixed as to whether employers value these courses, modules, certificates, and badges.

2. The Beauty College and the Technical College

1. Elise A. Couper, John P. Hejkal, and Alexander L. Wolman, "Boom and Bust in Telecommunications," *FRB Richmond Economic Quarterly* 89, no. 4 (2003): 1–24.

2. Brian O'Reilly and Ann Harrington, "Billionaire Next Door," *Fortune*, September 6, 1999.

3. Roger O. Crockett, "The Last Monopolist," *Bloomberg*, April 12, 1999.

4. Kim Strosnider, "For-Profit Higher Education Sees Booming Enrollments and Revenues," *Chronicle of Higher Education* 44, no. 20 (January 23, 1998): A36.

5. For a substantive discussion of these issues, see William Darity Jr. and Alicia Jolla, "Desegregated Schools with Segregated Education," in *The Integration Debate: Futures for American Cities*, eds. Chester Hartman and Gregory Squires (New York: Routledge, 2009), 99–117; Arthur H. Goldsmith, William Darity Jr., and Jonathan R. Veum, "Race, Cognitive Skills, Psychological Capital and Wages," *Review of Black Political Economy* 26, no. 2 (1998): 9; Karolyn Tyson, William Darity Jr., and Domini R. Castellino, "It's Not 'a Black Thing': Understanding the Burden of Acting White and Other Dilemmas of High Achievement," *American Sociological Review* 70, no. 4 (2005): 582–605.

6. Except for cosmetology certificate programs at not-for-profit community colleges, all cosmetology programs are for-profit although none of them are what we would call financialized—publicly traded and guided by acquisitions and degree expansion.

7. The empirical picture here on racial differences in wealth and income is so persistent it almost feels comical to cite them. Despite a slight narrowing during the pre-bust years of low unemployment, black–white–Hispanic wealth gaps favor whites. After the recession, those numbers are even starker: in 2010 the median white household was worth $141,900, 12.9 times more than the typical black household, which held just $11,000 in wealth. In 2007, the ratio was ten to one. The divide between white families and Hispanics was similar. See: Pew Research Center, http://www.pewresearch.org/fact-tank/2014/12/12/racial-wealth-gaps -great-recession. Also see Darrick Hamilton and William Darity Jr., "Race, Wealth, and Intergenerational Poverty," *American Prospect* 20, no. 7 (2009): A10–A12.

8. IMDb describes *Boiler Room* as a crime thriller about "A college dropout [who] gets a job as a broker for a suburban investment firm, which puts him on the fast track to success, but the job might not be as legitimate as it sounds." That illegitimate job is working as a day trader in a dark, cloistered office with dozens

of others selling questionable stocks. The room is the boiler room and the term is also a metaphor for the conditions that drive the protagonist to work there and the financial loopholes that make boiler rooms possible.

9. Many of those trash leads were accumulated from very old leads that had once been fresh. Others were culled from lead aggregators. Companies buy marketing data on prospective clients based on market research of their likely or ideal customer from lead generator and lead aggregation companies. These companies extract data on customers from a variety of sources, including online forms like those you might complete when you sign up for a website to read exclusive content or you fill out a sweepstakes entry form. If you reflect on how often you complete those and how honest you are when you do, you have a good idea of why these leads were trash: poorly validated contact information from someone who likely did not request any information about college then sold to for-profit (and some not-for-profit) colleges who then use enrollment representatives to convert them to paying students.

10. Researchers have primarily studied code-switching among black and Hispanic speakers. Especially in education research, there is a discussion about the extent to which code-switching is a cognitive and/or social tool that can impede or facilitate learning. See: Charles E. DeBose, "Codeswitching: Black English and Standard English in the African American Linguistic Repertoire," *Journal of Multilingual & Multicultural Development* 13, no. 1–2 (1992): 157–16; Marcyliena Morgan, "Theories and Politics in African American English," *Annual Review of Anthropology* (1994): 325–45; Lisa M. Koch, Alan M. Gross, and Russell Kolts, "Attitudes Toward Black English and Code Switching," *Journal of Black Psychology* 27, no. 1 (2001): 29–42.

11. Similarly, as a researcher I attended a U.S. Census data training program in 2014. Survey analysts with the Census Bureau had tested several questions to try to capture the school type workers attended to increase their labor market value. "For-profit" and "career college" did not test well enough (were not reliable or valid measurements) to be included in the survey questions.

12. Carolin Hagelskamp, David Schleifer, and Christopher DiStasi, "Profiting Higher Education? What Students, Alumni and Employers Think About For-Profit Colleges. A Research Report by Public Agenda," Public Agenda (2014).

13. "For-profit institutions for many decades also have accounted for the vast majority of enrollments in non-degree granting postsecondary schools (those offering shorter certificate programs) both overall and among such schools eligible for federal (Title IV) student financial aid" (Deming, Goldin, and Katz 2011).

14. See Rhonda Sharpe, Steve Stokes, and William Darity Jr., "Who Attends For-Profit Institutions? The Enrollment Landscape," in *For-Profit U* (Palgrave Macmillan, 2017), which I edited with William "Sandy" Darity Jr., for more on these enrollment patterns. Broadly, all research on the Wall Street era of for-profit colleges describes the students enrolled in four-year and graduate programs as less likely to be white, poor, or female than those enrolled in two-year or certificate programs.

15. David J. Deming, Claudia Goldin, and Lawrence F. Katz, "The For-Profit Postsecondary School Sector: Nimble Critters or Agile Predators?," *The Journal of Economic Perspectives* 26, no. 1 (2012): 139–63.

16. There is no shortage of research conducted or polemics written to explain, justify, or condemn this financialized corporate model of shareholder education. For various perspectives see: Daniel L. Bennett, Adam R. Lucchesi, and Richard K. Vedder, "For-Profit Higher Education: Growth, Innovation and Regulation," for Center for College Affordability and Productivity (NJ1) (2010); Johann N. Neem, Brenda Forster, Sheila Slaughter, Richard Vedder, Tressie McMillan Cottom, and Sara Goldrick-Rab, "The Education Assembly Line," *Contexts* 11, no. 4 (2012): 14–21; Richard S. Ruch, *Higher Ed, Inc.: The Rise of the For-Profit University* (Baltimore: Johns Hopkins University Press, 2003); William G. Tierney and Guilbert C. Hentschke, *New Players, Different Game: Understanding the Rise of For-Profit Colleges and Universities* (Baltimore: Johns Hopkins University Press, 2007); A.J. Angulo, *Diploma Mills: How For-Profit Colleges Stiffed Students, Taxpayers, and the American Dream* (Baltimore: Johns Hopkins University Press, 2016).

17. Exceptions are traditional residential colleges that have been purchased by for-profit college corporations, e.g., Grand Canyon University.

18. Asking if "federal student aid raises tuition" at for-profit colleges, superstar researchers Cellini and Goldin find that for-profit colleges that receive federal student aid have higher tuition than those that do not. This appears to work independently of the cost of operations or instruction. Instead, the price increase is related to the market's ability to pay and the federal government's maximum allowable subsidized dollars to be paid. Essentially, for-profit colleges are expensive because they can be (Cellini and Goldin 2014).

19. I make the distinction because there is also affirmative action for legacy applicants, athletes, and so on.

20. Sara Goldrick-Rab, *Paying the Price: College Costs, Financial Aid, and the Betrayal of the American Dream* (Chicago: University of Chicago Press, 2016).

3. Jesus Is My Backup Plan

1. Atlanta mayor William B. Hartsfield infamously called Atlanta a city too busy to hate in 1960. Hartsfield was making the point that although Atlanta was in the South, it would be too preoccupied with economic prosperity to get up in arms about racial grievances. Of course, Atlanta became a staging ground for the civil rights movement despite this declaration, but the moniker stuck.

2. Further to this point, I even reject moralizing about spending money on the conspicuous consumption of what economists call "visible goods," e.g., clothing, TVs, cars. The issue comes down to debt having some moral value attached. David Graeber's exhaustive anthropological history of debt in human history shares my position on debt itself being immoral and dismisses the idea that some debt is less immoral than others (David Graeber, *Debt: The First Five Thousand Years* [Brooklyn: Melville House, 2011]). It is a fiction. Yes, student loans have to be repaid. The terms of that debt—generous repayment options, for example—may be tied up in the idea that the money is being spent on a moral good. But, in fact, we are moralizing about how poor students use their student loan money. I may have missed them, but I cannot recall many screeds about Harvard Law School students using their student loan money to rent apartments or subsidize their summer travels, even though they do. Second, many have found that African Americans and Hispanics (groups often associated with the "immoral" act of spending their student loan money on nonessential goods) spend more on visible goods because they need those goods to signal to white gatekeepers that they aren't violent, low class, or dangerous. Morality around how students use their student loan money is a way to, as Graeber puts it, punish winners who aren't supposed to win. For various takes on this issue see: Kerwin Charles, Erik Hurst, and Nikolai Roussanov, "Conspicuous Consumption and Race," NBER Working Paper No. 13392, September 2007; Tressie McMillan Cottom, "Why Do Poor People Waste Money on Luxury Goods?," in *Poverty/Privilege: A Reader for Writers*, ed. Connie Snyder Mick (Oxford, UK: Oxford University Press, 2015).

3. For more on legislative history of how the calculation for total cost of attendance came to be, see Kim Dancy and Rachel Fishman, "A Legislative History: Why Is Cost of Attendance So Complicated?," for the New America Foundation at https://www.newamerica.org/education-policy/edcentral/more-than-tuition-2.

4. Robert Kelchen, Braden J. Hosch, Sara Goldrick-Rab, "The Costs of College Attendance: Trends, Variation, and Accuracy in Institutional Living Cost

Allowances," for the Wisconsin Hope Lab, 2014. Retrieved from http://www.wihope lab.com/publications/Kelchen%20Hosch%20Goldrick-Rab%202014.pdf.

5. See "Fast Facts About Higher Ed in the Atlanta Region," report from the Atlanta Regional Council for Higher Education, available at http://atlantahighered .org/Reports/FastFactsAboutHigherEducation/tabid/732/Default.aspx 2012.

6. Clark Atlanta University, Fort Valley State University, Interdenominational Theological Center, Morehouse College, Morehouse School of Medicine, Morris Brown College, Pain College, Spelman College.

7. Ibid.; Kresge Public Agenda survey.

8. Warren and Tyagi 2007; Jacob S. Hacker, *The Great Risk Shift: The New Economic Insecurity and the Decline of the American Dream* (Oxford, UK: Oxford University Press, 2006); Kalleberg 2011.

9. Sociologist Jesse Goldstein has written on the ideological construction of "entrepreneur" as a symptom of the globalization processes Hacker describes in *The Great Risk Shift*. UC Berkeley economists Ross Levine and Rona Rubenstein found that most entrepreneurs are white, male, and highly educated with inherited family wealth. Despite pronouncements that black women are the fastest-growing group of entrepreneurs, there are significant differences in wealth, access, scale, and success among entrepreneurs who are white and male and those who are not. That is true both of our imagined ideal (Silicon Valley tech geniuses versus home health-care business owners) and the reality in which minorities and women are more likely to start businesses that provide services.

10. Janelle Jones and John Schmitt of the Center for Economic and Policy Research published "A College Degree Is No Guarantee" in 2014. In it, they document what has been true for African Americans in the paid labor market since we have been allowed to participate in it: at every level of educational attainment, African Americans earn less than whites do. Jones and Schmitt specifically look at young workers with college degrees in the post-recession economy, or "new economy." They find that African Americans who make good on the education gospel not only earn less than whites with no college degree do, but also that they are more likely to be unemployed and underemployed, often in a job that doesn't require a degree. This is even true for those in the vaunted science, technology, engineering, and math (STEM) professions. This is paired with the historical and current reality that African Americans have always had approximately twice the rate of unemployment as whites, have negligible inherited wealth, and experienced the greatest loss of wealth during recessions of any group in the United States. Cumulatively,

this caused economists William Darity Jr., Darrick Hamilton, Anne E. Price, Vishnu Sridharan, and Rebecca Tippett to declare in their 2015 policy paper on race and wealth that "umbrellas don't make it rain." That is, studying and working hard—the prescribed "umbrella" for racial disparities—isn't enough for African Americans to close those disparities.

11. I will spare readers a dissertation on the origins and uses of the term "cultural capital." It may be good enough to know that it is an important social science term, credited to French theorist Pierre Bourdieu, and can potentially cause a fist fight at an academic dinner party. The term is used just enough in common parlance that it is also worth clarifying how I use it here. Quite literally, I mean the non-financial resources one has that promote upward social mobility, maintain social status, or possibly facilitate downward social mobility. Think about how encyclopedic knowledge of symphony music might make one popular at an elite country club, reinforcing to peers that one is "the right kind of people," but isolate one at a social event in an urban youth club. The students in Lower Ed are identified by schools and the public as having a certain type of cultural capital. For-profit colleges in the Wall Street era became efficient profit machines in large part because they catered to that cultural capital.

12. Rakesh Kochhar and Richard Fry, "Wealth Inequality Has Widened Along Racial, Ethnic Lines Since End of Great Recession," *Pew Research Center* 12 (2014). Retrieved from http://www.pewresearch.org/fact-tank/2014/12/12/racial -wealth-gaps-great-recession.

13. Laura Sullivan, Tatjana Meschede, Lars Dietrich, Thomas Shapiro, Amy Traub, Catherine Ruetschlin, and Tamara Draut, "The Racial Wealth Gap: Why Policy Matters," Institute for Assets and Social Policy, Brandeis University and Demos (2015). Also see latest from Oliver Shapiro and colleagues: Thomas Shapiro, Tatjana Meschede, and Sam Osoro, "The Roots of the Widening Racial Wealth Gap: Explaining the Black-White Economic Divide," Institute on Assets and Social Policy working paper (2013): 1–8. Retrieved from http://www.brandeis.edu /now/2013/february/wealthgap.html.

14. Darrick Hamilton, William Darity Jr., Anne E. Price, Vishnu Sridharan, and Rebecca Tippett, "Umbrellas Don't Make It Rain: Why Studying and Working Hard Isn't Enough for Black Americans," Insight Center for Community Economic Development, Oakland, CA. Retrieved from http://www.insightcced .org/report-umbrellas-dont-make-it-rain, accessed August 15, 2015.

15. Sandra E. Black, Paul J. Devereux, Petter Lundborg, and Kaveh Majlesi, "On the Origins of Risk-Taking," Working Paper No. w21332, National Bureau of Economic Research, 2015.

16. Manuel Aalbers, *Subprime Cities: The Political Economy of Mortgage Markets* (New York: John Wiley & Sons, 2012).

17. For one of the best meditations on race, the neoliberal logic of the new economy, and the resulting "hustle" see: Lester K. Spence, *Knocking the Hustle: Against the Neoliberal Turn in Black Politics* (Brooklyn: Punctum Books, 2015).

18. There are many historical and contemporary accounts of the systematic marginalization, underfunding, and sabotage of historically black colleges. Contemporary research from Marybeth Gasman, and historical work from James Anderson on the education of blacks in the U.S. South more broadly, are good places to start. Also, the legacy continues. In 2013, a federal judge ruled that the state of Maryland was perpetuating a segregated higher education system using enrollment strategies that undermined enrollment at historically black colleges.

19. American Council on Education, "Understanding College and University Endowments," policy report, 2014. For a more critical analysis of university endowments, see: Darrick Hamilton, Tressie McMillan Cottom, Alan A. Aja, Carolyn Ash, and William Darity Jr., "Why Black Colleges and Universities Still Matter," *The American Prospect*, November 9, 2015. Also, Astra Taylor has a good read on how universities with large endowments manage them in ways that aren't always consistent with offsetting student expenses or improving educational quality (Astra Taylor, "Universities Are Becoming Billion-Dollar Hedge Funds with Schools Attached," *The Nation*, March 8, 2016). Finally, for a good academic history of institutional wealth management, see Craig Steven Wilder, *Ebony and Ivy: Race, Slavery and the Troubled History of America's Universities* (New York: Bloomsbury, 2013). For the post–World War II context see Elizabeth Popp Berman, *Creating the Market University* (Princeton: Princeton University Press, 2011). The gist of all of this is that endowments are tied to all of the historical processes of wealth creation that are familiar to readers: slavery and colonialism, and later the military industrial complex, globalization, and scientific innovation. Some institutions have more such wealth than do others. Those with more wealth tend to use it in ways consistent with market logics like for-profit colleges use, but they also use a portion (albeit, a relatively small one) of that wealth to buffer economic downturns that make college more expensive for students who cannot gain admission to the

wealthiest universities. HBCUs are a special case of this, because racist public policies and the racist extraction of black wealth have made both the institutions and its likely students particularly vulnerable.

20. Ibid.

21. Ibid. For-profit college SEC documents. See Chapter 1.

22. The Education Commission of the States calls this mismatch between graduation requirements and college admissions criteria requirement misalignment. A database of the high school graduation requirements and the admissions requirements to the state college system can be found here: http://ecs.force.com/mbdata/mbquest7ne?Rep=AHC.

23. London is similar to many other poor women who make the seemingly irrational choice to have children that they cannot afford. Sociologists Kathryn Edin and Maria Kefalas's study of poor black, white, and Hispanic women in "Promises I Can Keep: Why Poor Women Put Motherhood Before Marriage" finds that women like London want children. And the futility of their upward mobility makes having a child more important to them and not less. Motherhood is an attainable social role with clear status and esteem. It doesn't require education or wealth to achieve. In contrast, marrying a poor man comes with risks that undermine women's happiness and stability. Poor women view childlessness as a tragedy and the lack of marriage as just one of the breaks.

24. Nicholas Hillman and Taylor Weichman, *Education Deserts: The Continued Significance of "Place" in the Twenty-First Century. Viewpoints: Voices from the Field*, Washington, D.C.: American Council on Education, 2016.

25. Brookstone closed its doors as I was writing this in May 2015.

26. Stephani Riegg Cellini and Claudia Goldin, "Does Federal Student Aid Raise Tuition? New Evidence on For-Profit Colleges," *American Economic Journal: Economic Policy* 6, no. 4 (2014): 174–206.

27. See Rohit Chopra's analysis of data on student loan defaults: "A Closer Look at the Trillion," Consumer Financial Protection Bureau policy brief, August 5, 2013. Retrieved from http://www.consumerfinance.gov/about-us/blog/a-closer-look-at-the-trillion.

28. I say "rarely" because as for-profit colleges have expanded to offer more doctorate degrees, the faculty in such programs often oversee and produce research. For example, Capella's Internal Review Board for research integrity looks very similar to those in traditional research universities: http://www.capella.edu/researchCenter/researchintegrity-office-at-capella.aspx. Still, it remains true that most faculty in

for-profit colleges are 1) not teaching graduate programs and 2) not incentivized to conduct academic research.

29. Cellini and Goldin put a finer point on this, saying, "We should note at the outset that few institutions [i.e., for-profit colleges who do not participate in federal financial aid programs] offer degree programs and almost none offers bachelor's and master's degrees" (Cellini and Goldin 2012).

30. Ibid.

31. The Institute for College Access & Success, "Quick Facts About Student Debt," policy brief, March 2014. Retrieved from http://ticas.org/sites/default/files /pub_files/Debt_Facts_and_Sources.pdf.

32. Goldie Blumenstyk, *American Higher Education in Crisis? What Everyone Needs to Know* (New York: Oxford University Press, 2014).

33. Jonathan Guryan and Matthew Thompson, "Report on Gainful Employment," Charles River Associates research brief, April 2, 2010.

34. For example, economist Anna Chung writes: "[S]tudents sort themselves into 4-year schools, community colleges and for-profit schools in descending order with respect to students' cognitive skills. We can then reasonably assume that the quality of these schools is commensurate with the corresponding students' cognitive skills." Anna Chung, "The Choice of For-Profit College," 2008. Working paper retrieved from http://citeseerx.ist.psu.edu/viewdoc/download?doi=10.1.1.690 .3567&rep=rep1&type=pdf, May 12, 2013.

35. Constance Iloh and William G. Tierney, "A Comparison of For-Profit and Community Colleges' Admissions Practices," *College and University* 88.4 (2013): 2. Iloh and Tierney's study of students' choice to enroll in a for-profit college rather than a community college gives descriptive statistics, including race. However, there is no discussion of how wealth or income or know-how is racially biased. There is a whole body of research about that very thing in the social sciences, but it is rarely applied to the phenomenon of for-profit colleges.

36. The Institute for Women's Policy Research, "Campus Child Care Declining Even As Growing Numbers of Parents Attend College," November 2014.

4. When Higher Education Makes Cents

1. William G. Tierney and Guilbert C. Hentschke, *New Players, Different Game: Understanding the Rise of For-Profit Colleges and Universities* (Baltimore: Johns Hopkins University Press, 2007).

2. Mitchell L. Stevens, *Creating a Class: College Admissions and the Education of Elites* (Cambridge, MA: Harvard University Press, 2009), 94.

3. Stevens 2009, 177.

4. Andrea Conklin Bueschel, "The Missing Link: The Role of Community Colleges in the Transitions Between High School and College" in *The Bridge Report: Strengthening K–16 Transition Policies*, Stanford Institute for Higher Education Research, 2013.

5. Annette Lareau's (2003) qualitative study of the home lives of middle-class and working-class children situates this institutional assumption within a broader social context of how social resources deliver students differently to different institutions. Annette Lareau, *Unequal Childhoods: Class, Race, and Family Life* (Oakland, CA: University of California Press, 2011).

6. Ann L. Mullen, *Degrees of Inequality: Culture, Class, and Gender in American Higher Education* (Baltimore: Johns Hopkins University Press, 2010); Jerome Karabel, *The Chosen: The Hidden History of Admission and Exclusion at Harvard, Yale, and Princeton* (Boston: Houghton Mifflin Harcourt, 2006).

7. Stevens 2009, 243.

8. The term "college valuation" refers to the complex set of values, aspirations, efficacy, and constraints that bind how students judge the rational costs and benefits of college attendance. Laura W. Perna and Patricia E. Steele, "The Role of Context in Understanding the Contributions of Financial Aid to College Opportunity," *Teachers College Record* 113, no. 5 (2011): 895–933.

9. Mullen 2010, 87.

10. "For Profit Colleges: Undercover Testing Finds Colleges Encouraged Fraud and Engaged in Deceptive and Questionable Marketing Practices," GAO-10-948T, Government Accountability Office, August 4, 2010. Available at http://www.gao.gov/new.items/d10948t.pdf.

11. Lydia Lum, "Handling 'Helicopter Parents,'" *Diverse Issues in Higher Education* 23, no. 20 (2006): 40.

12. Claire E. Ashton-James, Kostadin Kushlev, and Elizabeth W. Dunn, "Parents Reap What They Sow: Child-Centrism and Parental Well-Being," *Social Psychological and Personality Science* (2013).

13. Stevens 2009.

14. Claudia Buchmann, Dennis J. Condron, and Vincent J. Roscigno, "Shadow Education, American Style: Test Preparation, the SAT and College Enrollment," *Social Forces* 89, no. 2 (2010): 435–61.

15. Carolin Hagelskamp, David Schleifer, and Christopher DiStasi, "Profiting Higher Education? What Students, Alumni and Employers Think About For-Profit Colleges. A Research Report by Public Agenda," Public Agenda, 2014.

16. M. Fox, M., "Student Debt and Enrollment in Graduate and Professional School," *Applied Economics* 24 (1992): 669–77; Laura W. Perna, "Understanding the Decision to Enroll in Graduate School: Sex and Racial/Ethnic Group Differences," *Journal of Higher Education* (2004): 487–527; Marcus M. Stewart, Ian O. Williamson, and James E. King, "Who Wants to Be a Business PhD? Exploring Minority Entry into the Faculty 'Pipeline,' " *Academy of Management Learning & Education* 7, no. 1 (2008): 42–55.

17. Sociologists Marion Fourcade and Kieran Healy explore this relationship between credit scoring cultures and unequal access to public resources in their research. See Marion Fourcade and Kieran Healy, "Classification Situations: Life-Chances in the Neoliberal Era," *Accounting, Organizations and Society* 38.8 (2013): 559–72.

5. Where Credit Is Due

1. Sophie Trawalter, Kelly M. Hoffman, and Adam Waytz, "Racial Bias in Perceptions of Others' Pain," *PloS one* 7, no. 11 (2012): e48546.

2. For a discussion of transferability between sectors, see Sean Anthony Simone, "Transferability of Postsecondary Credit Following Student Transfer or Coenrollment," National Center for Education Statistics, Washington, D.C., 2014 policy brief. It's worth noting that the community college sector's transferability isn't ideal either (although the credits are less expensive and are potentially more legitimate). See David B. Monaghan and Paul Attewell, "The Community College Route to the Bachelor's Degree," *Educational Evaluation and Policy Analysis* 37, no. 1 (2015): 70–91.

3. Gregory Anderson, Jeffrey C. Sun, and Mariana Alfonso, "Effectiveness of Statewide Articulation Agreements on the Probability of Transfer: A Preliminary Policy Analysis," *The Review of Higher Education* 29, no. 3 (2006): 261–91.

4. See the Kaplan University website for an example of how they market their transfer policies. http://www.kaplanuniversity.edu/transfer-credits/community -college-students.aspx.

5. For example, the conference produced an edited volume: Tressie McMillan Cottom and William A. Darity Jr., eds. *For Profit Universities: The Shifting Landscape of Marketized Higher Education* (New York: Palgrave Macmillan, 2017).

6. Gaye Tuchman, *Wannabe U: Inside the Corporate University* (Chicago: University of Chicago Press, 2009).

6. Credentials, Jobs, and the New Economy

1. BLS data from http://www.bls.gov/ooh/personal-care-and-service/barbers-hairdressers-and-cosmetologists.htm.

2. 2014 tuition data was: $19,210 in tuition, $2,226 for necessary supplies or the "kit," which includes styling equipment. All of this could be financed in one's student aid. An additional $8,100 was projected for "personal expenses" like transportation. The total cost of anticipated tuition for the year-long certificate program was $29,536.

3. Haley Sweetland Edwards, "America's Worst Community Colleges," *Washington Monthly*, September/October 2013. Retrieved from http://www.washingtonmonthly.com/magazine/september_october_2013/features/americas_worst_community_colle046450.php.

4. Nidia I. Bañuelos, "From Commercial Schools to Corporate Universities: Explaining the Shift in Proprietary Business Education in the US, 1970–1990," *The Journal of Higher Education* 87, no. 4 (2016): 573–600.

5. In his study of the expansion of traditional higher education in the early twentieth century, David Brown argues that the nature of the labor market manufactured demand for credentials by *ex ante* linking credentials to desirable professional jobs.

6. David J. Maue and George Wilson, "Determinants of Declining Wage Mobility in the New Economy," *Work and Occupations* 42, no. 1 (2015): 35–72.

7. John Gapper, "Your Services Are No Longer Required," *The Future of Work Is Human*, August 8, 2016. Available at https://www.futureworkishuman.org/services-no-longer-required-part-2/#.

8. The discussion of shoring up the federal system of financial aid for these changes remains little discussed. See Frank Pasquale for a fuller discussion: Frank A. Pasquale, "Democratizing Higher Education," *Loyola Consumer Law Review*, forthcoming (2016).

Epilogue

1. From David Sarasohn, "The Republican War on Public Universities," *New Republic*, August 10, 2016.

2. See J. Boli, F.O. Ramirez, and J.W. Meyer, "Explaining the Origins and Expansion of Mass Education," *Comparative Education Review* 29, no. 2 (1985), 145–170, for an example of this kind of neo-institutional theory of educational expansion and D.P. Baker, "Forward and Backward, Horizontal and Vertical: Transformation of Occupational Credentialing in the Schooled Society," *Research in Social Stratification and Mobility* 29, no. 1 (2011), 5–29, for more contemporary criticisms of credentialing theory.

3. See Sarah L. Jaffe's excellent *Necessary Trouble: Americans in Revolt* (New York: Nation Books, 2016) on the history and trajectory of student loan debt organizers.

4. William Darity Jr. and Darrick Hamilton, "Bold Policies for Economic Justice," *The Review of Black Political Economy* 39, no. 1 (2012): 79–85.

5. Conrad De Aenlle, "Rebooting a Career, at a Technical School," *New York Times*, April 25, 2009. Available at http://www.nytimes.com/2009/04/26/jobs/26vocational.html.

INDEX

ABOUT THE AUTHOR

Tressie McMillan Cottom worked in enrollment at two for-profit colleges. After experiencing the kinds of choices students faced, she left the for-profit educational sector to go study it in graduate school. She is now an assistant professor of sociology at Virginia Commonwealth University. She has been a columnist for *Slate* and an online contributor to the *Washington Post* and *The Atlantic*, and is quite fond of Dolly Parton, fancy coffee, brunch, nineties hip-hop, bacon, and the Delta blues. She lives in Richmond, Virginia.

Celebrating 25 Years of Independent Publishing

Thank you for reading this book published by The New Press. The New Press is a nonprofit, public interest publisher celebrating its twenty-fifth anniversary in 2017. New Press books and authors play a crucial role in sparking conversations about the key political and social issues of our day.

We hope you enjoyed this book and that you will stay in touch with The New Press. Here are a few ways to stay up to date with our books, events, and the issues we cover:

- Sign up at www.thenewpress.com/subscribe to receive updates on New Press authors and issues and to be notified about local events
- Like us on Facebook: www.facebook.com /newpressbooks
- Follow us on Twitter: www.twitter.com /thenewpress

Please consider buying New Press books for yourself; for friends and family; or to donate to schools, libraries, community centers, prison libraries, and other organizations involved with the issues our authors write about.

The New Press is a 501(c)(3) nonprofit organization. You can also support our work with a tax-deductible gift by visiting www.thenewpress.com/donate.